Library of
Davidson College

Eric Hobsbawm
Ken Gill
Pete Carter
Kevin Halpin
Roger Murray
Digby Jacks
Mike Le Cornu
Royden Harrison
Stan Newens
Tony Benn
Steve Jefferys
Bob Wright
Bernard Dix
Hilary Wainwright
Jack Adams
Raymond Williams
Jack Jones
Robin Blackburn

The Forward March of Labour Halted?

edited by
Martin Jacques
Francis Mulhern

NLB

in association with
Marxism Today

This collection first published, 1981
© the collection, *Marxism Today* and Verso Editions & NLB

© Parts 1 and 2, *Marxism Today*
© in individual contributions remain with
their respective authors

© E.J. Hobsbawm, 1978, 1979, 1981

331.094
F745

**British Library
Cataloguing in Publication Data**
Hobsbawm, E.J.
   The forward march of Labour halted?
   1. Labor and laboring class –
   Great Britain
   I. Title
   335'.1'0941   HD8395

ISBN 0–86091–041–5
ISBN 0–86091–737–1 Pbk

Typeset in Monophoto Century Schoolbook by
Servis Filmsetting, Manchester

Printed in Great Britain by
Blackwell Press Ltd, Worcester

Verso Editions and NLB, 15 Greek Street, London W1

82-3808

Contents

Editors' Preface　　　　　　　　　　　　　　　VII
Notes on Contributors　　　　　　　　　　　　　XI

1

Eric Hobsbawm
The Forward March of Labour Halted?　　　　　1
Ken Gill
Pete Carter
Kevin Halpin
Roger Murray
Digby Jacks
Mike Le Cornu
Royden Harrison
Stan Newens
Eric Hobsbawm
Response

2

Tony Benn
An Interview with Eric Hobsbawm　　　　　　75

3　　　　　　　　　　　　　　　　　　　　101

Steve Jefferys
Bob Wright
Bernard Dix

Hilary Wainwright
Jack Adams
Raymond Williams
Jack Jones
Robin Blackburn

4
Eric Hobsbawm
Observations on the Debate 167

Editors' Preface

The depth of Britain's crisis is now almost universally recognized and felt. It is not only that we face the worst recession since the thirties, with some 3 million unemployed. Today, in contrast with that earlier period, the economy has no empire to depend upon and no centres of new industrial growth holding out the hope of overall regeneration in the future. At the same time, the crisis has created new social tensions, most vividly manifested in the rioting of the summer of 1981. And it has led to the break-up of the basic political consensus that dominated Britain for most of the post-war period, right into the late seventies. Seldom has Britain's political future been less predictable.

The election of the Thatcher government was a watershed. 1979 saw the return, for the first time, of a government pledged to undo the labour movement's most important gains: the commitment to full employment, the welfare state and a large public sector. Its objective, pursued via free-market economics and public expenditure cuts, is drastically to weaken the power and position of the organized working class. In these terms alone, the Conservative victory represented a very serious setback for the labour movement. The government offensive, together with the recession, has disoriented and demoralized the trade unions, whose present posture is in sharp contrast with the remarkable militancy that confronted the Heath government of 1970–74. But equally important was the sheer scale of the electoral reversal: Labour's share of the vote fell to its lowest level since 1931, marking the movement's most serious political defeat in nearly fifty years.

The defeat of 1979 and the policies of Thatcherism have unleashed a major debate in the Labour Party. This debate has already produced the most important constitutional changes since 1918, and it has seen the rise of a left more determined and effective than any in the party's history. However, these developments have opened deep internal fissures, which have already led to the formation of a new party, the Social Democrats, and there is mounting evidence of electoral instability.

Thatcherism itself now faces grave electoral problems, yet it is far from clear that Labour will reap the benefit of the Conservatives' difficulties. The labour movement is now in a profound crisis that affects not only its internal structures and policy alignments but also its popular electoral base. This crisis is not simply the creation of 1979: it goes back much further. What is at issue is the whole development of the labour movement in post-war Britain.

This book is a contribution to the current debates over the history, the present state and the undecided future of the labour movement. No such collection can claim to be comprehensive— the range of issues is far too wide. The main focus of the volume is on the trade unions and the Labour Party, and certain key aspects of their practice and perspectives. The individual essays will speak for themselves; but two distinguishing features of the book as a whole deserve mention here.

Chronologically, the debate spans the last year of the Callaghan government and the first two years of its successor. Hobsbawm's wide ranging analysis of the development of the working class and its organizations, and the discussions it provoked, anticipated themes that became widely current only after the debacle of 1979. The first phase of the debate unfolded in a climate of looming electoral defeat and renewed union militancy, and the latter is a major preoccupation throughout. Its later phases, post-dating the general election, reflect both a sharpened sense of political adversity and the heightening struggle in the Labour party. The book thus presents a record of continuous debate across three of the most critical years since the war. The debate is notable also for the diversity of its contributors. Politically, it embraces members of the Labour, Communist and Socialist Workers' parties, and also representatives of other socialist currents to the left of Labour. More important, perhaps, the book bridges the division of labour characteristic of most discussion on the left. It includes not only political actors but also representatives of the industrial, white-collar and public-sector unions, officials and workplace militants alike; not only those directly engaged in the struggles of the labour movement but also socialist academics and writers—all participants in a common discussion.

The essay that gives the coll its title, 'The Forward March of Labour Halted?', is the text of the Marx Memorial Lecture for 1978; it was first published in *Marxism Today* in September 1978. The response now reprinted, with a small number of minor editorial changes, in part 1 of the volume appeared in the same journal in the following sequence: Ken Gill, December 1978; and in 1979, Pete Carter, January; Kevin Halpin, February; Roger Murray, March; Digby Jacks and Mike Le Cornu, April; Royden Harrison, June; Stan Newens, July. Eric Hobsbawm's 'Response' appeared in the issue for September of that year. Hobsbawm's interview with Tony Benn took place in July 1980 in Birkbeck College London, at a public discussion arranged by the college's History and Politics Departments; a transcript of the discussion was published in *Marxism Today*, October 1980, and is reprinted here (part 2) in slightly different form. The eight essays of part 3 were commissioned specially for this volume; they were written at various times between August 1980 and May 1981, and all appear here for the first time. Part 4, Hobsbawm's 'Observations on the Debate', was written in late July 1981 and appears here for the first time.

We would like to thank Jon Bloomfield, Halya Kowalski and Margaret Mulvihill for their editorial assistance.

MARTIN JACQUES
FRANCIS MULHERN

Contributors

JACK ADAMS is convenor at British Leyland's Longbridge plant and secretary of the BL Combine Committee.

TONY BENN is the member of parliament for Bristol South-east, a member of the Labour Party's National Executive Committee, and the author of *Arguments for Socialism* and *Arguments for Democracy*.

ROBIN BLACKBURN is managing editor of *New Left Review*

PETE CARTER is Midlands regional organizer of the Union of Construction, Allied Trades and Technicians, and a member of the Executive Committee of the Communist Party.

BERNARD DIX is assistant general secretary of the National Union of Public Employees, and a member of the Labour Party's National Executive Committee.

KEN GILL is general secretary of the Amalgamated Union of Engineering Workers–Technical, Administrative and Supervisory Section, and a member of the TUC General Council.

KEVIN HALPIN is chairman of the Liaison Committee for the Defence of Trade Unions, a member of the Executive Committee of the Communist Party.

ROYDEN HARRISON is professor of social history at Warwick University; he has written *Before the Socialists* and edited *Independent Collier*.

ERIC HOBSBAWM is professor of history at Birkbeck College London; his numerous books include *Industry and Empire*, *Labouring Men*, *Revolutionaries* and *The Age of Capital*.

DIGBY JACKS is a divisional officer with the Association of Scientific, Technical and Managerial Staffs.

STEVE JEFFERYS is a former senior shop steward at Chrysler, Linwood; he is now in the National Union of Journalists, Freelance Branch, and is a member of the Socialist Workers' Party.

JACK JONES is a former general secretary of the Transport and General Workers Union.

MIKE LE CORNU is a shop steward at Heathrow Airport.

ROGER MURRAY was at the time of writing a shop steward at British Leyland's Solihull plant.

STAN NEWENS is the Labour member of parliament for Harlow.

HILARY WAINWRIGHT is co-author of *Beyond the Fragments* (with Sheila Rowbotham and Lynne Segal) and *The Workers' Report on Vickers* (with Hugh Beynon); she has also contributed to *State Intervention in Industry: A Workers' Inquiry* (Coventry, Liverpool, Newcastle and North Tyneside Trades Councils).

RAYMOND WILLIAMS has written, among many books, *The Long Revolution, Television: Technology and Cultural Form* and *Keywords*, and edited *The May Day Manifesto*; he is professor of drama at Cambridge University.

BOB WRIGHT is assistant general secretary of the Amalgamated Union of Engineering Workers, Engineering Division.

MARTIN JACQUES is editor of *Marxism Today*, the theoretical and discussion journal of the Communist Party.

FRANCIS MULHERN is on the editorial committee of *New Left Review*.

1

The Forward March of Labour Halted?

Eric Hobsbawm

It is my privilege to give the Marx Memorial Lecture of 1978 and I want to use it to survey some developments in the British working class during the past hundred years. It is a long-established habit, on these occasions, to take the texts of Marx and Engels as our starting point, but I shall not do so for two reasons. In the first place, as it happens, neither Marx nor Engels said much about the British working class between the end of the First International and the 1880s, and to the best of my knowledge they said nothing whatever about it exactly one hundred years ago. In fact on this very day (17 March 1878) there appeared in an American journal one of a series of five articles by Engels on the European workers. This mentioned numerous countries from Russia to Portugal, but contained not one word about Britain. He remained totally silent—no doubt regretfully silent—about the admittedly uninspiring labour scene in this country a century ago. In the second place, and more to the point, what I wish to underline is something which a Marxist analysis alone will help us to understand, but which Marx's texts cannot; that the forward march of labour and the labour movement, which Marx predicted, appears to have come to a halt in this century about twenty-five to thirty years ago. Both the working class and the labour movement since then have been passing through a period of crisis, or, if you prefer to be mealy-mouthed about it, of adaptation to a new situation. Most of us, engaged in day-to-day struggle, have not paid as much attention as we ought to this crisis, though we can hardly fail to be aware of some of its aspects. My purpose is to see it in the long-term perspective of the changing structure of British capitalism and the proletariat in it. I see our task as marxists, and mine as the Marx Memorial Lecturer, as applying Marx's methods and general analysis concretely to our own era, and I hope Marx himself would also have seen it that way.

A Working-class Majority

It was taken for granted in the 1870s that the great majority of the British people consisted of manual workers and their families—and this meant manual workers outside agriculture. I need hardly add that the majority, even of the farming population consisted of proletarians, that is, of wage-labourers. In both these respects Britain was then peculiar and probably unique: in the enormous size and percentage of its manual working classes and in the relatively small size and percentage of its agricultural population, and above all its insignificant peasantry. This had some significant political consequences, which are still in some ways felt. Whereas in most other states at that period the introduction of a democratic voting system would still have left the manual workers in a minority, in Britain, so it was believed, they would immediately constitute a majority. In 1867, the statistician Dudley Baxter estimated the non-agricultural manual workers at just under 70 per cent of the population. So, from the point of view of the ruling classes, it was absolutely essential to gain or maintain the political support of an important section of the working class in one way or another. They could not hope to offset an independent class-conscious party of the proletariat by mobilizing the majority of peasants, petty craftsmen and shopkeepers, whether with or against the working class. They had to come to terms with the fact of a working-class majority from the time of the Second Reform Act onwards.

Decline of Manual Occupations

I shall leave aside for the moment the question whether what was understood by 'manual workers' in the 1860s and the 1870s is what we would today call a working class or proletariat. However, whatever they were, they got their hands dirty, and for most of the past century the manual workers in this broad definition have not grown but declined. In 1911 they included about 75 per cent of the population, in 1931 about 70 per cent, in 1961 64 per cent and in 1976 a little over half.

This does not, of course, mean that the percentage of proletarians in the technical sense has gone down, that is, of people who earn their living by selling their labour-power for wages, plus their dependants. On the contrary, in this sense proletarianization has, as Marx predicted, continued to increase. We cannot accurately measure the percentage of 'employers and proprietors' for the nineteenth century, but in 1911 it included less than 7 per cent of the occupied population and it has since gone down—after staying more or less stable until 1951—to something like $3\frac{1}{2}$ per cent in the middle 1960s. So we have, over this century, growing proletarianization combined with the relative decline, within the wage-earning population, of the manual workers in the literal sense of the word.

This is a very general phenomenon in the industrial countries. However, in Britain the decline is particularly striking for a special historical reason. A hundred years ago the sector of white-collar work in the widest sense employed only a tiny number of wage-earners; probably relatively less than in other countries with a substantial bureaucracy, public and private. For instance, in 1871 'commercial occupations' as a whole, occupied less than 200,000 out of about 12 millions, whereas by 1911 it already included about 900,000. By 1976 about 45 per cent of the occupied population could be classified as non-manual.

Here, then, is the first major development of the past hundred years. But let us look more closely at the manual workers. A hundred years ago industry depended on manual labour to an extent we find difficult to grasp today, since the technology of the industrial revolution which Britain pioneered, and which made this country into the 'workshop of the world', was, by modern standards, extremely undeveloped; it was in fact, as Raphael Samuel has recently reminded us, a 'juxtaposition of hand and steam-powered technology'. It was, to use the modern term, enormously labour-intensive. Craft skills of the kind associated with the pre-industrial artisans, were no doubt to some extent supplemented or speeded up by power and machinery, but they were not yet to any extent replaced by it. Not until the end of the century were automatic machine-tools seriously introduced into British engineering workshops. Other operations, skilled or less skilled, relied almost entirely on manpower. Practically every ton of coal—which supplied the overwhelming bulk of power for all purposes—was got by men with picks and shovels.

Two Consequences

These characteristics of nineteenth-century British production had two consequences. In the first place, growth of output was linked to an expansion in the workforce to an extent that is difficult to recall today. Thus between 1877 and 1914 the tonnage of coal produced in British pits just about doubled—and so did the number of coalminers. On the eve of the First World War something like one and a quarter million men (plus their families) were required simply to produce Britain's coal. Today the spectacularly larger energy requirements of Britain, including coal, oil, gas, electricity and nuclear power, do not require more than a fraction of this enormous labour force. The army of labour was constantly growing. But in the second place, the relative backwardness of mechanization by twentieth-century standards gave the British worker whose manual skill and experience was indispensable—and this included others besides apprenticed craftsmen—considerable strength in collective bargaining. British trade unionism was therefore already strong or potentially strong, even in industries in which, elsewhere, it was notoriously weak, as in cotton mills. Unionism was recognized by government a little more than a century ago, and—leaving aside particular areas and industries—no systematic and consistent attempt to smash it as a whole was made thereafter, or succeeded for any length of time. At the same time, the peculiar structure of British trade unionism also reflected—and still reflects—this historic past.

Pattern of Union Organization

Thus, unlike many other countries, our unions are not a small number of giants each covering in theory all workers within a specified industry. Though this pattern of industrial unionism was favoured, and at one time militantly advocated, by the socialists, it was not generally successful. Even on the railways, as we know, the rivalry between industrial and sectional unions has not been eliminated. Instead—or rather side-by-side with such industrial tendencies—we have the coexistence of craft unions and, a phenomenon peculiar on this scale to Britain, the great 'general unions' which gradually absorbed those not eligible for, or wanted by craft unions, those too weak to form them, and a variety of others. Furthermore, in some ways this tendency, which was first established in the period of the great dock strike of 1889, continues to reassert itself. Smaller unions have increasingly tended to amalgamate into bigger ones; but while these amalgamations could be seen, in the first half of the present century, as steps towards a sort of industrial unionism, in the past twenty years they have looked increasingly like the formation of new conglomerates of the 'general union' type—as with the merger of the AUEW with the foundrymen and the draughtsmen and the ETU with the plumbers. Conversely, the enormous potential strength of the 'craftsman' type of worker continued to be felt in unionism, particularly in the great complex of metalworking, engineering and electrical industries that went on expanding as the old nineteenth-century industries of mass employment, such as textiles, mining and transport, contracted. When mass unionism came to these industries in the 1930s and during the war, it was initially through the craftsmen—often, as in the aircraft industry, men who still worked, and sometimes thought, in the old terms of craft pride. As late as 1939 the men at Harland and Shorts in Belfast still refused to accept piece-rates, as their grandfathers had done in the craft unions of Marx's day. These were the men who spread unionism into the motor industry; who kept the average engineering factory as a collection of separate craft unions, and, incidentally, who sent the women and the non-craftsmen to be organized by the T&GWU, which has thus become the majority union in the motor industry. And, incidentally, this persistence of multiple unionism in so many factories made rank-and-file inter-union co-ordination by such people as shop stewards so formidable a force on the British industrial scene.

Historic Transformation

I have stressed these historic continuities. But they are combined with one major historic transformation. A century ago the working class was deeply stratified, though this did not prevent it from seeing itself as a class. The very people who were the backbone of trade unionism, perhaps with the exception of the miners, were, and were seen as, a labour aristocracy which looked down on the mass of those whom it regarded as unskilled, 'mere labourers'. But industrial change first threatened and then eroded this superiority from three directions. In the first place the rise of tertiary employment—white-collar and professional employment—produced a new form of labour aristocracy which identified directly with the middle class. It is only since the Second World War—at least outside the public sector—that the white-collar workers and professional workers have organized as a mass in trade unions, and increasingly within the TUC, that is, the conscious labour movement. In the second place modern technology increasingly created a stratum of professionals and technicians separately recruited from outside rather than promoted from those with workshop experience. So the gap between the labour aristocracy and the middle strata widened. On the other hand modern technology and industrial organization threatened the privileged position of the labour aristocrat, by increasingly turning him into, or replacing him by, the less skilled process worker operating specialized machines, or carrying out specialized parts of an increasingly elaborate division of labour. In other words, as Marx had predicted and as the capitalists always intended, skill was increasingly transferred from men to machines or to the design of the flow of production. In fact the labour aristocracy was threatened with dilution. Thus the labour aristocrats were not only forced further away from the middle strata, but closer to the other strata of the working class, although their economic advantage (as distinct from their position in the social structure) was not seriously weakened before the First World War. They tended to be radicalized, especially in the great complex of industries in which mechanization, mass production, and similar changes in the organization of industry produced the most direct confrontation between the skilled worker and the new threats, in the growing complex of the metalworking industries.

Now I would like to note, in passing, that my explanation of this process is a little different from Engels, though it does not actually conflict with it. Engels, who wrote about these problems in the 1880s (notably in the new Prefaces to his *Condition of the Working Class*), stressed two things: the formation of a 'relatively comfortable' and ideologically moderate labour aristocracy in Britain, and the world monopoly of British industrial capitalism which provided benefits for *all* British workers, though disproportionate ones for the labour aristocracy. But 'even the great mass had, at least, a temporary share now and then' (Preface 1892, *Marx & Engels on Britain*, p. 31). He expected a radicalization of the British working class as a result of the decline in the British world monopoly, but he did not foresee this happening among the labour aristocracy of the 'old unions', but rather by the emergence of labour-organization among the hitherto unorganized masses, whose minds were 'free from the inherited "respectable" prejudices which hampered the brains of the better situated "old" Unionists' (p. 32). What he did not appreciate sufficiently were the developments in capitalist production that were to radicalize the former labour aristocracy itself, at any rate in the growth industries of the twentieth century. But in the 1880s these were not yet very visible.

A Common Style of Proletarian Life

All this does not mean that the working class became a single homogeneous mass, although in many ways it was drawn more closely together, by a growing class consciousness, by political demands that united workers of all strata and sections—for instance, in the fields covered by local government, of education, of health and social security—by a common life-style and pattern, and, for a minority, of labour and socialist ideology. This common 'style', if I may so call it, of British proletarian life, began to emerge just about a century ago, was formed in the 1880s and 1890s, and remained dominant until it began to be eroded in the 1950s. I am thinking not only of the rise of the socialist movement and the Labour Party as the mass party of British workers, the changes in trade unionism, the enormous and unbroken increase in the number of co-op members from half a million in 1880 to three million in 1914, but of non-political aspects of working-class life; of the rise of football as a mass proletarian sport, of Blackpool as we still know it today, of the fish-and-chip shop—all products of the 1880s and 1890s, or at the earliest the 1870s; the famous cap immortalized by the Andy Capp cartoon, which is, broadly speaking, Edwardian; and a little later— they had hardly developed much before the First World War—of the council flat or house, of the picture palace, of the *palais de danse*.

Changes in British Capitalism

At the same time the nature of British capitalism has changed profoundly, in four ways. First, as suggested, it has been transformed as a system of production by technology, mass production and the enormous concentration of the productive unit, that is, the plant in which people work. In 1961 about half of all workers in manufacturing establishments worked in plants of more than 500 workers, about a quarter in establishments over 2,000, less than 10 per cent in units of fifty or under. Second, the rise of monopoly capitalism with a massive public sector has concentrated employment even more, and in particular created a huge sector of government and other public employees such as simply did not exist a century ago. Today something like 30 per cent of all people work in the public sector—as employees of government, local authorities, nationalized industries—and the proportion is rising. That is to say, for every two people employed in the private sector (I omit employers and self-employed) there is now roughly one in the public sector. Third, it follows that the factors which determine the workers' conditions are no longer, to any major extent, those of capitalist competition. The capitalist sector is no longer one dominated by the free market, since it is largely monopolized; and the public sector, both as an employer, as the provider of all manner of social services and payments, and as the manager of the economy, very largely determines them, or at least the limits within which they are fixed. Political and not profit decisions determine it. And fourth, the actual standard of living of most workers has been revolutionized for the better. Several of these trends can be traced back to the period between Marx's death and the First World War, but the really dramatic transformation has occurred since 1939.

This has implied a number of changes within the working class, quite apart from the growing division between a manual working class which increasingly tended to vote for its class party and a white-collar stratum which, at least outside the public sector, was predominantly conservative, until in the last twenty years or so it has also begun to organize itself on trade unionist lines, and—perhaps to a lesser extent—to turn politically leftwards. I shall mention some of them.

Women Workers

First, the organized working class a hundred years ago was almost entirely masculine, as Engels himself noted; except in the textile industry. Insofar as women worked for wages, they did so primarily before and after marriage (in 1914 only about 10 per cent of married women were so employed) and were regarded as unskilled and treated as cheap labour. The largest by far—44 per cent in 1881—in any case worked as servants. Even in 1911, when service had already begun to decline as an occupation, there were still a million and a half maids. That was the 'Downstairs' of 'Upstairs and Downstairs'. Though there was already a remarkable influx of women into industry, and even more into office work and shop work in the quarter-century before 1914, women continued to be, and still continued to be, treated only too often as a sort of second-class worker, and the demand for equal pay did not make any serious headway until after the Second World War. And though the employment for wages of married women increased a little between the wars—in 1931 13 per cent of all married women were so employed—the practice did not become normal until after the Second World War. Since 1951 the number of married women technically described as 'occupied' has gone up from about one-fifth to about half. This is a major change in the composition of the working class.

Immigration and the Working Class

Geographically, the working class a century ago was, in spite of all migration and mobility, a collection of localized communities. It is still locally rooted to a much greater extent than the middle classes, as anyone can tell as soon as a trade unionist from Birmingham or Gateshead, not to mention Clydebank or Swansea, opens his or her mouth. But, on the whole, such local differences did not run counter to the sense of a single class consciousness, but were part of it. The differences between Lancashire and Yorkshire workers did not prevent—they may even have underlined—their common characteristics as workers. Even the growing differences—especially between the wars—between the old nineteenth-century industrial areas of the North, of Scotland and Wales, and the new industrial areas of the Midlands and the South-east, did not produce greater division of feeling and attitude. The one exception to this was nationality (or in the case of the main immigrant group, the Irish, nationality-cum-religion). Here, as Marx himself had realized, there was a force that did deeply split the British working class, at least potentially, as witness the political history of Merseyside. And if the rivalries between the supporters of Sheffield United and Sheffield Wednesday, of Notts. County and Notts. Forest, did not so much divide as underline the basic unity of workers in those cities, we all know that the supporters of Rangers and Celtic, or Liverpool and Everton, of Hearts and Hibs., divided on national religious lines. Still, the striking thing about the British working classes is, how little—I would say how increasingly little—they were affected by such national splits until the 1950s, in spite of the very obvious fact that Scotsmen, Welshmen and Irishmen were proudly conscious of *not* being Englishmen; and the other way round. Unlike, say, the Poles in imperial Germany, the Irish in Britain, if organized at all, joined the all-British unions and supported the all-British party of their class, at all events after Ireland had become independent. Until the labour movement as a whole entered upon its present crisis, there was no significant mass base for national parties in Scotland and Wales, and until the mass immigration from the former empire after the Second World War one would have said that working-class racism was probably less significant in Britain than, say, in France—even allowing for anti-Irish, and from the early 1900s, some localized anti-Jewish feeling. If anything, it looked like being a declining force for three-quarters of a century after 1878. Here is another significant and unwelcome development of the past quarter of a century.

Sectional Differences

But there are other divisions within the working class. A hundred years ago there were three main sectional differences within the working class: between industries and particular branches, firms or localities in an industry (Tyneside and the South-west); between various grades and levels of workers ('craftsmen' and 'labourers'); and between rival groups within the same level or grade, as between different groups of the skilled. As to the first, local and regional differentials were high and probably growing a hundred years ago; but have tended to diminish since 1900, though at times when some regions were relatively prosperous and others very depressed as between the wars, they could remain very large in practice because of unemployment. In theory the rise of state monopoly capitalism and employment in the public sector has also tended to even them out. In practice things are more complicated. This is not the place to discuss these problems in greater detail.

Demarcation

As to sectional differences between rival groups of the same level, these have a long history. They caused conflicts chiefly when groups tried to keep a monopoly of particular jobs for themselves against others, either because technical progress undermined their natural monopoly of long training and skill, or because in times of unemployment there was more pressure to fill a limited number of jobs. Thus bitter demarcation disputes in the north-eastern shipyards reached a peak in the 1890s, and this industry and area is still familiar with them. As the old division of labour became technologically obsolescent, such rival or potentially competing groups of specialized workers have often tended to amalgamate—the merger of the boiler-makers, shipwrights and blacksmiths, for example—but this kind of sectionalism is far from dead. Indeed it has increased inasmuch as modern industrial development cuts across trade sectionalism and makes it possible for different industries or groups of workers to carry out what are essentially the same or alternative processes. Thus in 1878 there could be no overlap between, say, compositors and journalists, but with modern technology that enables a journalist to type straight on to the press, there can and is. Containerization produces potential and actual conflicts between dockers, lorry-drivers and railwaymen which simply did not and could not exist in 1878 or even much later. And so on. Some coalminers would prefer the shutting down of the nuclear power industry, but workers in that industry presumably would not. Hence I would suggest that this type of sectionalism, probably after a period when it tended to decline, has been on the increase since the Second World War, and this is a dangerous development.

Stratification

The third kind of sectionalism, stratification, was kept largely out of sight a hundred years ago, for two reasons. First, the favoured strata (such as the so-called labour aristocracy) were still rather successful at restricting entry to their trades or keeping themselves in a favoured position by being, on the whole, the only ones with access to effective organization. In fact, there is little doubt that at that period unionism reinforced exclusiveness. Only in the period of socialist leadership, at first very slowly, but more rapidly from the great labour unrest before the First World War, did trade unions come to be factors for evening out rather than for increasing local, trade and grade differentials. Second, a hundred years ago wages and conditions were still largely fixed by custom and convention, and only partly by pure market calculation. The bourgeoisie paid as little as they could, but even when they could afford to, thought there ought to be a ceiling above which worker's wages should never rise, and they could think so because workers thought in terms of 'a fair day's pay for a fair day's work', depending on the sort of workers they were. Their limit was a lot lower than the sky. Now neither of these observations is any longer true. The old hierarchies have been undermined by technological change and differentials have been eroded, particularly by the development of complex, not systematically planned, opaque and unpredictable changes in wage-payment, which no longer give an automatic advantage to skill—payment by results, systematic overtime, and some of the effects of productivity bargaining. And (especially in the great boom period after the Second World War) the workers learned that the limit of their demands is a lot nearer the sky than most of them ever imagined, and the employers were willing to make concessions they would have regarded as unthinkable earlier. These tendencies can, I think, be traced back to the Edwardian period, for they can be detected in some syndicalist arguments.

A Growth of Sectionalism

Now all this suggests that the old working-class stratifications should lose their significance, and—with all the survivals of old divisions and tensions—common working-class interests should increasingly prevail. And this probably happened in the first half of this century. But it would be a mistake to think that this has made the working class more homogeneous. On the contrary, it seems to me that we now see a growing division of workers into sections and groups, each pursuing its own economic interest irrespective of the rest. What is new here is that their ability to do so is no longer related to traditional criteria such as their technical qualifications and standing on, as it were, the social ladder. In fact it now often happens not only (as sometimes occurred even a hundred years ago) that groups of workers strike, not minding the effect on the rest—skilled men on labourers, for example—but that the strength of a group lies not in the amount of loss they can cause to the employer, but in the inconvenience they can cause to the public, that is, to other workers by power blackouts or whatever. This is a natural consequence of a state-monopoly capitalist system in which the basic target of pressure is not the bank account of private employers but, directly or indirectly, the political will of the government. In the nature of things such sectional forms of struggle not only create potential friction between groups of workers, but risk weakening the hold of the labour movement as a whole. The sense of class solidarity may be further weakened by the fact that the real income of a family may no longer actually depend on a worker's own job alone, but even more on whether their wives or husbands also work and what sort of jobs they have, or on various other factors not directly determined by the union struggle. In short, though there are plenty of material and moral reasons for solidarity, and a few dramatic recent examples of it—as over the Industrial Relations Act in 1970–71 and the miners' strikes—there is not much doubt that sectionalism is on the increase.

The Poor

There is one final division within the working class, which in some ways recalls the divisions of a hundred years ago, though conditions are quite different. It is between those who could take full advantage of the great economic and social improvements of the postwar era and those who could not—if you like, those who would, a century ago, have been called 'the poor'. There are the people in persistently low-paid occupations virtually beyond the range of effective trade unions. There are the quarter of all households that get more than half their household income from social security and earn less than £40 a week; the people who live in private rented accommodation as against those who own houses and rent council housing; in 1975 17 per cent of unskilled workers were private tenants as against 11 per cent of skilled workers; the poor who live worse and pay more. And when we consider these, let us not forget that, by international standards British wages have fallen behind others, and the British social security system, of which we were so proud in the immediate postwar years, has probably fallen even further behind the social security systems of several other European countries. It is the poor who are disproportionately worse off, and whom the established modes of labour organizations help least directly. A hundred years ago the labour movement recommended its forms of struggle and organization to everybody—trade unions, co-ops, et cetera. But it was then not *accessible* to everybody, but only to favoured strata of workers. Let us ask ourselves whether there is not a similar complacency among some sections of the movement today.

Class Consciousness

Now how far does the development of class consciousness of the British working class reflect these trends? Let us take the most elementary index of it, trade unionism. This undoubtedly increased pretty steadily from a century ago, though we have no comparable figures before the 1890s: say from 13 per cent of the labour force in 1900 to 45 per cent just after the Second World War (1948). But thereafter it remained stagnant for quite a bit, or even dropped a little, and though it grew in the 1960s and 1970s, it is now only a little higher (as a percentage) than in 1948—46 per cent. And—a point we don't often note—it is much lower than in Denmark, Sweden and Belgium, where it is around 70 per cent and actually a little lower than Italy. Now of course the composition of trade unionism has changed—there are a lot more women and white-collar workers—but the point I wish to note regretfully is that 35 per cent of the employed are not in any trade union, and that this percentage has not declined for thirty years. And also, that Britain, the home of mass trade unionism, has clearly fallen behind some other countries.

Declining Vote

If we look at the political expression of class consciousness, which means in practice, support for the Labour Party, the picture is even more troubling. The number and percentage of Labour voters (including Communist ones) grew without interruption (except for 1931) between 1900 and 1951 when it reached a peak of 14 millions or just under 49 per cent of all votes. After that it went down to 44 per cent in 1959 and 1964, rose again to just over 48 per cent in 1966 and then fell again. At the 1974 election it was well under 40 per cent. What is more, in *absolute* figures Labour (plus Communist) after 1951 barely ever got to within one million of its then vote, and in 1974 it polled about $2\frac{1}{2}$ million less than in 1951, less than in *any* election since 1935. Of course this trend also affected the Conservatives who reached their all-time peak ($13\frac{3}{4}$ million) in 1959, but that is no consolation.

There is no equally simple way of measuring the highest degree of class consciousness, namely socialist consciousness, but if we are to take the active membership of all socialist organizations as a very rough criterion—as distinct from trade union activism—then I also suspect that from some time after the early 1950s there is a decline, perhaps broken in the late 1960s. However, a very high proportion of the new socialist activists inside and outside the Communist Party and other Marxist groups, in this most recent period, have probably been not manual workers, but students and white-collar or professional workers. Of course we ought to note that until the 1950s very many, and perhaps most, of these new socialist activists, often from working class and white-collar families, would not have been able to go to colleges.

Marx and Engels

So it seems to me that for the first seventy years or so of the last century, Marx and Engels would have been neither very surprised nor very disappointed by the tendencies of development in the British working class. Not very surprised, because the tendencies were such as they predicted, or might have predicted, on the basis of Marx's own analysis of the development of the factory system, for example; though I think they would have been a bit surprised by the speed with which the tertiary sector developed, though perhaps not so much by the formation of a new conservative white-collar labour aristocracy. They would not have been very disappointed by, because they did not expect very much from the British working class beyond what actually looked like happening, the growth of a mass political party based on class consciousness, separate from the parties of the bourgeoisie, and increasingly if vaguely committed to replacing capitalism by socialism. Of course, like you and me, Marx and Engels might well have wanted the British working class to be a bit more revolutionary and, like you and me, they would have been pretty contemptuous of the Labour leadership, but things did look like moving in the right general direction. But in the past thirty years this movement seems to have got stuck, except for one trend: the 'new' labour aristocracy of white-collar technical and professional workers has become unionized, and the students and intellectuals—from whom it is largely recruited—have also been radicalized to a greater extent than before.

The Avoidable Crisis

I have already suggested some of the developments in the economic and social structure of the country and its working population which might explain this. But Marxists are not economic and social determinists, and it simply will not do to say that this crisis of the working class and the socialist movement was 'inevitable', that nothing could have been done about it. We have already seen that the halt in the forward march began even before the dramatic changes of the past twenty years; that even at the peak of the 'affluent society' and the great capitalist boom, in the middle 1960s, there were signs of real recovery of impetus and dynamism: the resumed growth of trade unions, not to mention the great labour struggles, the sharp rise in the Labour vote in 1966, the radicalization of students, intellectuals and others in the late 1960s. If we are to explain the stagnation or crisis, we have to look at the Labour Party and the labour movement itself. The workers, and growing strata outside the manual workers, were looking to it for a lead and a policy. They did not get it. They got the Wilson years—and many of them lost faith and hope in the mass party of the working people.

Economist Militancy

At the same time the trade union movement became more militant. And yet this was, with the exception of the great struggles of 1970-74, an almost entirely *economist* militancy; and a movement is not necessarily less economist and narrow-minded because it is militant, or even led by the left. The periods of maximum strike activity since 1960—1970-72 and 1974—have been the ones when the percentage of pure wage strikes have been much the highest—over 90 per cent in 1971-2. And, as I have tried to suggest earlier, straightforward, economist trade union consciousness may at times actually set workers against each other rather than establish wider patterns of solidarity.

So my conclusion is that the development of the working class in the past generation has been such as to raise a number of very serious questions about its future and the future of its movement. What makes this all the more tragic is that we are today in a period of world crisis for capitalism, and, more specifically, of the crisis—one might almost say the breakdown—of the British capitalist society, at a moment when the working class and its movement should be in a position to provide a clear alternative and to lead the British peoples towards it.

We cannot rely on a simple form of historical determinism to restore the forward march of British labour which began to falter thirty years ago. There is no evidence that it will do so automatically. On the other hand, as I have already stressed, there is no reason for automatic pessimism. Men, as Marx said (the German word means men and women), make their history in the circumstances that history has provided for them and within its limits—but it is they who *make* their history. But if the labour and socialist movement is to recover its soul, its dynamism, and its historical initiative, we, as Marxists, must do what Marx would certainly have done: to recognize the novel situation in which we find ourselves, to analyse it realistically and concretely, to analyse the reasons, historical and otherwise, for the failures as well as the successes of the labour movement, and to formulate not only what we would want to do, but what can be done. We should have done this even while we were waiting for British capitalism to enter its period of dramatic crisis. We cannot afford not to do it now that it has.

Ken Gill

It was a rare pleasure to read a clear, readable analysis of the trends within the labour movement in *Marxism Today*. Hobsbawm, in 'The Forward March of Labour Halted' was spotlighting the major question facing socialists today. Unfortunately he got it all wrong. Confusing definitions of the speed of advance are inevitable from one who asserts 'The capitalist sector is no longer one dominated by the free market' and 'Political and not profit decisions determine it.'

A Picture of Advance

Any historian must have a reliable measure of left advance or retreat. By almost any recognized criteria his conclusions were wrong. If leadership is the criterion the movement has shifted to the left since Hobsbawm's halcyon days of the 30s and 40s. Can you really compare the Joneses and Scanlons with the Lawthers and the Deakins? If industrial struggles are the test there were few successful strikes in the period following the General Strike; and, as today, they were also 'economist' by the definition which appears to be adopted by Eric Hobsbawm. Economism as defined by Lenin was a denial of the need of political as well as industrial struggle. Trade unions today embrace political objectives sometimes to the detriment of their members' economic interests. The problem which faces the left is to make those political objectives socialist.

The policies proposed by the capitalist establishment in the

30s and 40s were supported without question by the TUC. Not so today. The article misinterprets the nature and effect of wages struggles in contemporary Britain. John Gollan, reviewing the period 1961–74 in Allen Hutt's *Short History* said 'There can be no doubt that the last decade of struggle proved and is proving itself one of the most momentous in the history of British trade unionism.' He had previously described the strengthening of the rank and file movement and the growing *political* activity of the movement.

Martin Jacques, in *The General Strike*, said: 'In contrast to 1926 the miners, *this time backed by the trade union movement*, refused to be diverted. In the process the Conservative Government fell . . . and the miners' demands were met' (my emphasis).

It disarms us to lose historical perspective because of the last four frustrating years when the right appeared to have gained some ascendancy.

1970–74

The retreat of the left was due to the acceptance of the Social Contract, a political bargain. Despite this temporary setback, the movement is stronger now than at any time in its history. The fight back against the Social Contract's restrictions has begun. The wage battles that are now growing will, through militancy, challenge contemporary capitalism.

Eric Hobsbawm concedes my point, 'At the same time the trade union movement became more militant. And yet this was, *with the exception of the great struggles of 1970–74* (my emphasis) an almost entirely economist militancy.' He then quotes strike figures for 1970–72 and 1974 and notes with obvious regret that these were *pure* wage strikes. So the exception to 'economist militancy' turns out to be a period of intense wages struggle! But he was right first time. Strikes that take place against legal sanctions for wage increases forbidden by law are not mere 'economist militancy'. His claim is like a characterization of the first half of the twentieth century as peaceful with the exception of the periods 1914–18 and 1939–45!

Wages Struggles and Political Change

It was precisely during the 60s and 70s period of mass *political* struggle, when 'wage militancy' was at its peak, that the ruling class tried a final solution of the trade union question. There is a clear link between struggle and political change. The fact is that wage struggles are no longer *pure* wage struggles. How can they be, in an era of state monopoly capitalism and government-imposed wage restrictions? In this context the demand consistently supported by the Communist Party, for the restoration of free collective bargaining is a profoundly political one.

The development of a militant wage *movement* is our first priority. These are the lessons of 1970-74.

The recent period has illustrated the breadth of the working-class struggle. The fights against closures, occupations, work-ins, battles for union recognition, political challenges such as the illegal strike attempt by the postmen against South Africa and the equal pay strikes, all show a more mature political level than the past. The lack of a mass struggle against unemployment is a direct result of trade union leaders' demand for *political* solidarity with right-wing Labour.

Lastly, there is the development of the Social Contract itself. Here a number of politically progressive demands were proposed as a *quid pro quo* for wage restraint. These demands did not come out of thin air; they arose from the struggles during the period which Hobsbawm writes off as being one of narrow-minded economism. Trade unions mistakenly traded in the wages struggle and naïvely expected a Labour cabinet to meet its social commitments. This would have required a massive challenge to the system, and the will and intent was absent in the leadership.

For many of the left it was a tragic error from which painful lessons are at last being learned. The Communist party did not make this error, although a careful reading of the party's press would show that Hobsbawm is not the only communist to be trapped by a simplistic analysis of the wages struggle over the last few years.

Qualitative Advances

Hobsbawm spends much of his article with a quantitative analysis of trade union membership and Labour Party voting figures. He almost ignores the qualitative changes which have occurred in the movement: (i) the growing strength of the shop stewards movement, of trade union and class organization at the point of production; (ii) the growing unionization and involvement of women in the movement; (iii) the development of policies within the trade unions on a broad range of economic, social, cultural and international questions (such as democratically-elected, legally-backed health and safety representatives; the battle against pay beds; state pensions; industrial support for Chile); (iv) the great advance, at a policy level, represented by the 1974 Election Manifestoes of the Labour Party.

The historic task facing our movement is to establish the working class as the leading force in British society. Recent history shows that, far from the 'forward march of labour' being halted, substantial advances have been made along this road. Organized labour is now a political power in the land and therefore the main enemy of the rulers of Britain; it cannot be swept aside as it was between the wars.

Pete Carter

Eric Hobsbawm's article and Ken Gill's reply afford the left the possibility of beginning an overdue debate, both on the period 1968–74 and on the whole question of the relationship between wages and trade union struggles and a strategy for socialist advance in a highly developed capitalist democracy.

It is also important because beneath the question is the problem of why the movement subsided so quickly after Labour came to power, and why it has not recovered since. The need to clarify problems relating to this period gain further urgency from the fact that we may now be standing on the edge of a new surge in wages and trade union struggle, renewed inflation, and a possibly worsened economy.

I think Hobsbawm's article begins to highlight a major problem confronting the labour movement. I found it fascinating reading and could relate its essence to the day-to-day struggle.

I often sit and ponder about the last twenty years of struggle. It is true that during this period there have been some enormous class battles, some major confrontations, and actions, which repeatedly confirm the power and strength vested in the working class and its organizations.

But while on the one hand we have witnessed this enormous activity, one must ask the question why are we no further forward in winning political advances. There can be no doubt that people in the material sense are better off today (though one must not ignore the abundant poverty still around) but where has it got us?

What is good about Hobsbawm's contribution is that it helps situate today's struggles in an historic perspective, and in so doing highlights some of the poverty of these struggles. The ruling class in Britain have been able to manipulate history in a way that perpetuates their own existence. This has been at the expense of a developing consciousness of the working-class movement and to a large extent restricts its ability to both come to terms and to understand the complex problems of current politics.

Wat Tyler, John Ball, Jack Cade and the men of Kent, Cromwell, the Levellers and Diggers, the Chartist movement, the experiments of Robert Owen, the beautiful contribution of William Morris, Tom Mann and the early campaigns on industrial unions, the rural struggles of 'Captain Swing', the formation of the Labour and Communist parties, are just a few of the battles of yesteryear that point to a richness in our forefathers carrying many lessons for us today.

Not to draw from the sum total of struggles denies present and future generations the ability to understand the class changes that are taking place, the ever-growing dangers of sectionalism within the working class and the reasons for instinctive rather than a developed class consciousness. For me Hobsbawm widens the area for trade union intervention in the revolutionary process and Ken Gill's response I find rather inadequate, narrow, certainly not helpful in the situation which we are now in.

The Arguments

Let us examine some of the arguments. Both contributions raise a number of general as well as specific points. First, there is the general one of the speed of the advance or retreat of the labour movement, especially since 1968, and the causes of it. Hobsbawm's answer is that the Labour Party and the Communist Party have continued in their long postwar decline.

Gill's response is that the left is stronger and the working class more militant. Both come to their conclusion by looking at the evidence in different ways. Hobsbawm comes to his by looking at the evidence of political choice and behaviour, while Gill assumes that the number and nature of strikes in the 1970–74 period is evidence itself of a leftward shift.

Neither seems totally satisfactory though the first seems more convincing than the second, and the incompleteness of the conclusions reached by these spokesmen in the party reflects the difficulties and uncertainties that we face.

The second general point raised is the type of relationship that exists between wages and political struggle. All too often assumptions are made about this relationship because there is little evidence that the struggles of 1968–74 had any lasting politicizing effect.

Too often we substitute, as Gill has done, a certain kind of wishful thinking which says that because we see struggle as political the mass of workers do also. In addition it should be remembered that the wages struggle is only one part of the class struggle and that at certain times some types of wages struggle may be politically self-defeating.

This is why one despairs when Gill says that the restoration of the wages movement is the key area of struggle, without any concrete suggestions as to how it is related to either the political struggle of the left or other areas of struggle like what is the relationship between the fight for wages and the struggle over investment policy, the problems of workers' control, or whether products are socially useful or not.

The constant assumption is that *all* wages struggles are good and politically progressive for the workers. Apart from the positive role of the wages struggle, it should also be remembered that at the political and ideological level they can often legitimate capitalism, confirming the 'law of the market' and the economic drowning of the working class's least defended sections. Where, for example, have the big manual unions been on the cuts in public expenditure and the campaign on low pay?

Gill seems to argue the view that to continue fighting for wages will see the eventual downfall of capitalism, and that militancy around this issue is enough. It is my view that nothing could be further from the truth. As a matter of fact I would go so far as to say that current wages struggles in isolation from political perspectives could create great divisions among the working class. The Ford workers' recent wages victory will (and should) be welcomed by the more advanced shop stewards as an important step forward, but the vast majority of British workers see it in terms of higher prices and a reduction in their standards—and see the Ford workers as the reason, and not the system. We ignore such problems at our peril.

There are other issues equal to that of wages that must be fought. Neither wages nor militancy are in themselves enough to make inroads in bringing about a more equitable organization of society. I make this point after many years of involvement in the wages struggle and from an assessment of the value of this alone, compared to the possibility today of uniting the wages issue with issues of a broader nature.

The Building Industry Experience

I can only reflect on my own industry and my immediate experience which although in embryo indicate more potential for revolutionary change.

The episode began in 1975 when Jack Munday, an Australian Communist Party member and past secretary of the Builders Labourers Federation, visited Britain. It was a very new experience to listen about a wider contribution Australian building workers were making to the political scene.

The whole development behind the Builders Labourers Federation was that of the need to make a wide contribution to the development of society through using its industrial muscle. Closely linked with environmental groups, the BLF stopped property speculators developing bush land, curtailed the building of speculative office blocks, helped to preserve communities whose homes were under threat of demolition, halted the construction of a power station, stopped the demolition of historical buildings which ranged from pubs to pulpits, while at the same time it was able to secure for its members the highest ever awarded wage increase. The BLF saw no contradiction, say, between using its strike weapon on a university extension on which the powers that be were denying women a course on femininism, and homosexuals entry because of their sexual orientation, and that of the wages struggle. In reality both struggles were essential and on both they were victorious.

My own union, UCATT, in the Midlands has begun to see struggle in wider terms and during the past four years has clearly identified with all sections of the community in struggle and participated with them.

Its role in campaigning to save a Victorian Post Office, its opposition to speculative office blocks, the campaign within its own ranks encouraging workers to demand that their labour be used in a socially useful way, the fight to save direct works departments linked to the campaign for public ownership of the industry around the slogan 'build for people and not for profits', has won for the union not just a wider appreciation for the role of trade unions from a wider section of the community, but more so an understanding of its own role.

It has been able to make the leap from pure wages struggle to identify with The Conference of Socialist Planners, The New Architecture Movement, the Anti Nazi League and Campaign Against Racism and Fascism, tenants movements and a whole variety of struggles that by and large are struggling against aspects of capitalism, but not yet fully conscious of the system. Friends of the Earth, Conservation and Victorian Societies, the Green Ban Action Committee, Hazards at Work group, Transport and Energy 2,000 movements all see in UCATT a source of strength aimed at helping them fulfil their aspirations. Neither is it all one way, because UCATT gains strength and confidence through association. Involvement with wider sections of society helps to develop and raise its consciousness, helps it to get a deeper knowledge and a wider view: broadens its horizons and helps it to achieve an all-round approach, caring for the community's problems.

In no way does this approach weaken the union: on the contrary, it makes better fighters of its members because it gives confidence and knowledge, and wins other forces to the fight for change. It is a natural and essential alliance that is tackling capitalism on many fronts, and the clarity and unity won from joint struggles helps the growth of an understanding of the complications of the issues initially involved. It is my belief that only through such a strategy can we begin to raise class consciousness.

A Shift to the Left?

The third general point that is raised is the important one of the shift to the left. Here Gill and Hobsbawm are in direct disagreement. The shift to the left has been spoken about in the party press from the end of the 60s and to some extent reflected a real change. However, the party has been inadequate in looking at the problems in any satisfactory way. Generally what it has been taken to mean is the movement covering the Labour Party leadership, the parliamentary Labour Party and a number of trade unions.

Now this has undeniably happened and should not be underestimated. But the real nature of the shift remains largely a mystery. What elements are available to allow us to penetrate it? Hobsbawm appears to be correct when he says that the numerical decline of the Labour and Communist parties and the vote reflects the sentiment of the average voter. 1970–74 was an exceptional period in the labour history of the postwar period which *appears* to have led to the development of a new, politically more advanced cadre in the labour movement, but what their number and quality is, is hard to gauge.

Partly in contradiction to this, there is plenty of evidence that the mass of the trade union membership has not significantly shifted to the left. It should also be remembered, that with the exception of a few unions, the left is most entrenched in those unions where there are no direct elections. On many issues in the trade union movement over the last few years, there is plenty of evidence of the leaders being to the left of the membership. The last element, stressed by Gill and largely missed by Hobsbawm, is the growth of democratic political struggles such as the pay beds issue, forms of radical struggle that have yet to be sufficiently integrated into an overall left strategy.

Since Ken Gill carries by far the most day-to-day responsibility in the labour movement the main reply must be to his contribution. I was disappointed because he did not face up to Hobsbawm's criticisms of sectionalism and racialism in the working class movement. I was also concerned about his overestimation of trade union leaders. Sure Jones was better than Deakin, but the complete omission by Gill of the importance of the rank-and-file contribution leaves him wide open to the criticism of a bureaucratic conception of left advance.

Throughout Gill confuses trade union organization with political understanding. On his definition we don't need political parties, just trade unions clashing with the state, and in no way did he convince me that the left is stronger than ever, the only evidence he offers is of something that might happen in the future.

My view is, for what it's worth, that Communists, trade unionists and the labour movement in general need to do some new thinking. I honestly believe the arguments advanced by Gill are the very reasons why the progressive movement is in decline and to base our future strategy on these thoughts will go to perpetuate rather than arrest the decline.

Hobsbawm does come to terms with the problems and based on his contribution we can map out a strategy of advance. And the first thing must be to turn the movement on to the offensive. All too often our actions are from a defensive posture.

A Broad Front

The working class and its organizations have enormous democratic strengths. Surely we need to use these strengths, free collective bargaining—yes, but over everything.

In other words our industrial muscle needs to be used in order to defend and improve the conditions of the weaker workers. The most powerful should stand side-by-side with the lower paid. Joint action needs to be taken, the annual conference resolution is not enough. We should be demanding a freeze on price rises. It would be possible to get workers to down tools over price rises but all too often this level of struggle is overlooked.

A broad movement should be worked for to stop cuts in public expenditure. The cuts have intruded into all aspects of our life. What is the point of trade unionists fighting for health and safety at work on the one hand, and on the other tolerating cuts in the hospital service, in education and in housing.

It seems a contradiction to me fighting for the right to work while at the same time negotiating the best possible redundancy payments. But very little is done to combat the ideology of redundancy payments, and the lack of a fight over this issue means acceptance of selling jobs, and more school leavers on the dole.

Most trade union leaders seem to be caught in a technological trap. They call for more investment in industry (today this means less jobs) but never ask, investment in what? The philosophy of jobs at any cost is a bankrupt one and reflects a low level of political thought.

The Lucas Aerospace corporation plan is of immense value in this respect. Its demands over production and not just distribution add a new dimension to trade union struggles. Their approach to the problem is an illustration of the maturity that has developed since the days not so long ago when workers were smashing up threshing machines.

The corporate plan is the product of workers looking at their industry, questioning what is produced, and putting forward alternative socially useful products. It is this sort of initiative that the wider community responds to.

Creative Marxism

Industrial and political struggle, it should be remembered, involves only a fraction of the working population, and there is only the most tenuous connection between the relative handful of militants and the overwhelming bulk of the workforce. It is this strategic majority that has got to be won, and we need a policy for them as well as for the advanced sectors, if not, any wage advance will be short lived. Meanwhile, the ruling class, because of the massive influence that it exercises over organized as well as unorganized labour, will be able, as after 1975, to negate at the political and strategic level, the small advances which have been won.

Hobsbawm's contribution is much broader in its approach and makes history a living reality. Not only does it help to map a way forward from historical experiences, but its insights aid our party's programme, *The British Road to Socialism*.

The need to broaden the campaigns of the labour and trade union movement is in essence the creative Marxism of our generation and is certainly continuing the struggle in the tradition of the great past masters who never lost sight of linking the vision or the gleam of communism with the day-to-day struggles.

It is now within our reach to build a broad democratic alliance in which the working class will fulfil its leading role. But this position is not automatic, it must be won, and the wages struggle on its own will in no way begin to implement the concepts within *The British Road*.

Kevin Halpin

Eric Hobsbawm's 1978 Marx Memorial Lecture was a timely attempt to assess, on the basis of Marxism, the current position of our labour movement. I make no apology for writing on this subject three months after the article appeared for I am in the same position as many in the labour movement; heavy commitments and little time for writing. This is a problem that the party must address itself to, if we are to avoid limiting participation in the discussion of the theories and policies of our movement of those who are in the thick of carrying them forward in the labour movement.

The proposition 'the forward march of labour halted' ignores the advances made. Can we as Marxists use the term 'halted'? The movement goes forward, but maybe not down a preconceived road. Yet, if as Marxists we start with a conception of what the movement ought to have done, then we start on a non-Marxist basis.

The article refers to a change in capitalism and the shrinking of private industry and concludes that this means that the public sector determines wages and conditions. This would mean that the economy is dominated by some state apparatus outside the capitalist spere. But the position of society today is that Marx's and Lenin's theories of the state hold good. The role of multinationals (not mentioned at all) is such that the overall domination of policy by the IMF and Common Market agencies may look like government operation and control, whereas government control such as the incomes policy is really the government operating on behalf of the multinationals.

Whatever the government of the day, for both Tory and Labour governments have a common ideological basis—the need to make capitalism viable—very little pressure need be exerted by the multinationals for government to intervene on their behalf and to squeeze out jobs, productivity, cut social services, and prevent any advance in living standards. Profit factors are not, as Eric says, secondary to political factors but control politics.

The Public Sector

It is obviously not correct to say that the public sector determines the limits set, for private firms such as Ford and British Oxygen have made the pace, although there is a new phenomenon in the way the government has used public funds to defeat any fight in the public sector. But there are those sections within the public sector who have the muscle to affect the profitability of capitalism as a whole, and then enormous concessions are made under many guises, such as productivity deals, which pushed up the money of miners and power workers. (Deals which were never monitored.) Such deals have not been confined to traditional sections but include power engineers and aircraft controllers, that is to say new sections who have the muscle and power. The weakness has been that there are large sections of public employees who are not able to exert this sort of pressure, and the present state of the British labour movement is such that all battles are fought by these individual sections—such as nurses, hospital ancillary workers, teachers, firemen, et cetera. The consequent isolation often leads to defeat and disillusionment to fight another day.

This explains the situation which Hobsbawm feels indicates a growth of sectionalism. But there is no need for this to be accepted as a future trend. The main problem, of course, is the inability of the trade unions to act in solidarity, for the role of the TUC to date has been at best to give a paternalistic nod of approval to action, but not to initiate united action.

Advances have been made but they have been countered by capitalism, which also changes its tactics. The big motor industry fights, led by Communists in unity, to prevent redundancies often had a mixed success. Yet they led to a whole change of attitude which it was necessary to achieve. For example, it was no longer accepted as a 'law of nature' that when the foreman tapped you on the shoulder and said 'you'll have to finish up and we'll let you know when the work picks up', you then spent an hour cleaning and grinding your tools and went. Defeating this led to the new attitude of the 'right to work', which was the central slogan of the fight at Upper Clyde Shipbuilders. But the capitalist class could see the challenge and met it by forcing through measures. First they got government payments under the Redundancy Payments Act and then, where the militancy was strong, they raised these payments so that a docker was getting £9,000 and a print worker £15,000. This was selling jobs for more money than any working person would ever see—short of winning the pools.

This then led to a cut in jobs and job opportunities for youngsters. We must reach a position that the trade union movement fights for a policy that jobs are not the property of individuals but of the trade unions. The social pressure for jobs for youngsters may be a good unifying issue, but all too often it has not been fought by those in work. The whole trade union movement must insist that vacancies be filled and back this action if necessary.

Other trends over this period have been the increasing nationalization of industry that capitalism through lack of investment has bankrupted. And with this, another new phenomenon has emerged. Capitalism has conceded, or as with ship repair has insisted on, nationalization to get cash compensation for otherwise unprofitable enterprises. They have changed their tactics, but live to fight another day. This can be clearly seen in the attempts to sell off profitable sections after the injection of public funds, as at Ferranti and the campaign to break up British Leyland. Where nationalization has occurred the companies have continued to operate in the same style as capitalist industries, as with BL and the Speke closure; all the lip service paid to consultation did not save Speke or stop the agreed loss of 7,000 jobs. Yet, applying Marxist theories to these situations, advances can be seen, but more needs to be done to fight for the control not only of nationalized and publicly-owned industries but also for their extension.

Any government could have made out a case for nationalization and proved it worked, had they cut prices instead of declaring colossal profits made by electricity, gas and telephones. But the anti-nationalization forces took the offensive and turned the argument on its head. They no longer said that nationalized industries always make a loss, they were now able to maintain that they put up your prices in order to make an enormous profit at the consumer's expense. Goverment strategy provided those opposed to nationalization with a gift of a case.

The Recent Period

In assessing the period from 1970–74 and the militancy that he refers to as 'great struggles' Hobsbawm ignores their political result. A tremendous page of history was written by the miners. It was the first time that class action had removed a government in office, and showed the correctness of our slogan 'Out with the Tories.' This mass pressure was countered by the whole weight of the capitalist state machine and by politicians who could see parliamentarianism endangered—the parliamentarianism of putting a cross on the ballot paper every five years. They realized at Saltley Gate what a weapon mass solidarity on the picket line was.

Solidarity for weaker sections will become more and more the order of the day for, unlike Eric, I do not believe that the strength of a group depends on the inconvenience it can cause the public, but on the effects on profitability. Such solidarity actions will bring to the fore the strike-breaking tactics of the police, and in this context it will be more essential to question the role of the TUC for without an all-round trade union action we cannot defeat these attacks.

In the lull throughout the labour movement our explanation of the state machine is one of our biggest weaknesses. It can only be done by a Marxist party injecting its theory into the labour movement. With the ending of many of the bans and proscriptions over this period many barriers to Communists working in this way have been removed and given us this opportunity.

The article correctly estimates the shrinking of industry in Britain, but this industry is tremendously profitable and is the key to the economy which is a capitalist economy. That is to say, one that relies on the exploitation of workers by hand and brain to produce surplus value. This shrinking of the working class in traditional industries does not present any major change in the direction of our work. We have not won the traditional working class for our overall policies. Very often in this discussion of new trends and forces there is a tendency to play down the amount of work needed in these traditional bases. The discussion frequently presents a picture of thousands of Communists searching for a factory gate with leaflets and papers to put across our policy. The opposite is the case—thousands of factories, pits, sites and depots are crying out for our policy and no one is there to put the case.

The forward march of labour has not been halted, in the changing face of capitalism advances have been made—but not as rapidly as we need. After the return of Labour in 1974, policies were started which could have made big advances. The Labour Party and the TUC have been won for advanced policies—the next stage is how are they to be implemented. This can only be done if those who pay the piper call the tune and the trade unions who finance the Labour Party insist on getting the policies they and their members pay for.

Roger Murray

Hobsbawm's article was timely and relevant. Perhaps its weakness was that it analyzed the labour movement somewhat in isolation from other elements of the social formation. Nonetheless it was very useful.

There *is* a political right shift in Britain, one that has been well described by Stuart Hall (*Marxism Today*, January 1979). The labour movement is not effectively challenging this political shift at the moment, although that is not to decry those activities presently taking place. Social democracy still dominates the labour movement. In trying to resolve Britain's economic problems, as Hall says, the government has to attempt to discipline its own class base if it is to accommodate the needs of capital. Support for the Labour Government wanes among the working class. The revolutionary element of this class has made little political headway. The Tories, with their right-wing populism are appearing as an alternative to Labour among large sections of the working class. The key problem that confronts the Communist Party is the task of winning the support of the working class, and in so doing, to unite it and win the support of other sections of society. Crude attempts to capture leadership by winning union positions in the absence of a mass base have failed. Our lack of a mass base has sometimes led our trade union activists to oppose the postal vote in union elections primarily because of the influence of the media in such elections. This has handed the 'democratic card' to the right wing to flaunt. Our job is to improve our mobilization of and communication with the trade union membership. Indeed, where this has been done, left wingers no longer fear the postal vote.

Sectional Differences

Leadership (or hegemony) cannot be won without putting demands that transcend, overcome, sectional differences. It is the duty of our party to search for such demands. The fight for them can win a mass base in the labour movement which is bound to be reflected in the leadership of the trade unions, Labour Party, et cetera. Action on such demands is a prerequisite to real left unity.

Without doubt the alternative economic strategy contains most of the basis for such demands. Vast potential for struggle exists around price control, restoring cuts in social services, the control of investment, import controls, more control at work, et cetera. Coupled with, linked with, the wages struggle, these demands could help unite the labour movement and win allies among other sections of society. The wages struggle *in isolation*, conducted *sectionally*, can and does divide the labour movement, isolate it from other sections and assist the right-wing drift for more law and order, more control over the unions. But the wages struggle will go on, regardless. Our job is to link it with wider demands and struggles. I think the denunciation of wages struggles as economistic, in vogue with some comrades, while being accurate in some ways, is unhelpful. Such denunciations are not understood. They serve only to confuse or enrage those already active in struggle. Our job is to win workers to widen their struggles, to offer *practical* and *political* assistance, not to sit back and pass judgement.

At the time of writing (January 1979) around 93 per cent of wage claims have been settled within the 5 per cent government pay guidelines. But the media concentrates on the lorry and rail strikes screaming 'chaos' and abusing pickets. The social service low-paid workers are being mobilized and the government is already making some tiny concessions to them.

It is possible, even probable, that we are faced with the return of the Tories.

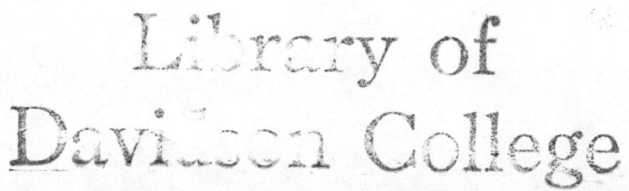

However, even under the Tories it will be equally important that wage claims are linked with wider demands for government action. This would help mobilize the movement around political issues and help set the stage for the election of a Labour government committed to challenge the power of the multinationals and their political support. For such a development, the intervention of the Communist Party is indispensable. Right and left social democracy have proved unable to frame policies capable of uniting the movement. Remember the left and their confusion over the Social Contract. Frankly, it would mean the party becoming more clear and united on the many issues that confront us.

The Need for Clarity

For instance, take three key questions: prices, investment and import controls. The party calls for a six-month freeze on prices. This is impractical. We must identify which section of the market we wish to control. Our main target must be the monopolies (private and public). But it is in the private sector that the greatest pressure for price increases exists (overheads, investment costs, wages, profit-maximization, et cetera). The private monopolies and multinationals and their control is the key to price control and to control over the economy. These must be our targets for both economic and political reasons. It is not the small shopkeepers who are the cause of rising prices, we must not attack that section, but win it from monopoly-capital's hegemony.

Confusion seems rife over the question of investment. Are we for or against more investment in British industry? Of course, we are for ridding ourselves of boring dirty jobs by the use of advanced technology. But are we posing the question of control over investment and the question of where the Communist Party thinks investment should be directed? Put bluntly, we have hardly tackled the question. Leyland comrades are for more investment in Leyland, as I hope is the rest of the party. But what of other industries? And can we say we have properly tackled the question of conditions of work when linked with new investment. Voluntary redundancy has proved a powerful challenger to the 35-hour week.

What of the restructuring of our economy in accordance with the demands and needs of the people, against the destruction of industry by the multinationals. Do we need a motor-cycle industry, should we expand the production (and cut the cost) of push bikes? I hope both answers are yes, but have we discussed it thoroughly?

Import controls are absolutely essential to balance our economy throughout any programme of investment and to retain key sections of our economy. We cannot allow the multinationals to dictate what happens to our economy. The drivel peddled by the ultra-lefts about exporting unemployment is unrelated to today's multinational domination of the world capitalist system. Do they want the socialist countries to allow the multinationals complete freedom to interfere with their economies? The technical advances under capitalism are causing unemployment everywhere. One control over this is import controls. We need to specify what we wish to control by how much and how long for.

Our challenge to capitalism and social democracy needs to be more thorough-going than even the above. We must challenge them at their very roots. More control and information over work is fundamental to advance. More involvement in locality struggles is the key to enabling the movement to shake off their ideological and actual control over people's everyday lives.

I will illustrate my argument with some examples. In Leyland, 'participation' has given the movement fore-knowledge of management plans if not the ability to change them. Some criticism exists about the structure of participation, but the principle is not in question. Slowly the movement is developing a long- and short-term alternative to the management's strategy. As yet though there has not been the conviction to transform these alternatives into a mass campaign. In addition there is recognition that the movement needs to be won to an understanding of the key role that Leyland plays in the British economy. But again there has been an inability to recognize the potential of a mass campaign on this issue as yet.

More positively, in my own constituency in Sparkbrook the party played the key role in establishing a broad committee to campaign on jobs. Residents' associations, trade unions, designers, councillors, lawyers, political parties et cetera, have all combined to campaign on *specific* proposals on the use of land to create employment. Approaches are being made to local and national government for funding. In making specific proposals and proving they could work the campaign has become meaningful, concrete and not just a set of abstract slogans (a common feature on the left).

It is interesting to note the response of the Labour group. Some councillors are fully supporting the campaign (and note the chairman is a well known Communist in the area) and some are obviously less keen. The controversy is over democracy and control. The mass support for the plans among residents and the labour movement will be the determining factor of whether these quite practical proposals are adopted.

If this campaign succeeds it will mean the labour movement *and allies* will have struck a real blow at unemployment and ruling-class hegemony precisely by its ability to mobilize masses around concrete demands in an area 'normally' closed to the labour movement.

At the time of writing an all-Midlands jobs campaign is being mobilized. It too has similar perspectives. If it begins to succeed this will mean an important shift in the ability of the labour movement to fight back.

Finally, this discussion must continue, drawing from the practical experience of those involved in struggle. In that light I think it would be helpful if false polarizations were avoided and serious debate continued. This would really help the forward march of labour.

Digby Jacks

Eric Hobsbawm's review of the recent history of the British labour movement is much to be welcomed. An historical attitude and perspective regarding the trade unions, the central core of the movement, is essential. It is a highly readable and thought-provoking account. But in its broad canvas, certain points are missed and arguable assertions made.

There is an implicit assumption that industrial unionism leads to working-class unity and greater combativeness. This needs to be argued through, and though the proposition is, I am sure, theoretically sustainable, practice speaks differently. In the area of the growing white-collar unionism, to 'force' these new trade unionists into existing industrial union moulds would be to re-enact the legend of Procrustes—and result in a weakening of trade unionism. The specific problems that face TASS in the amalgamation could be magnified many times. It is my experience in this area that there is a greater staff affinity in a union context on a plant or company basis. The industrial cohesion is often weaker for staff, particularly those who are professionally qualified across industrial boundaries. The Federal Republic of Germany has seventeen industrial unions with very clear dividing lines. Postwar experience does not indicate a growth of industrial militancy or political consciousness there. No doubt there are many reasons for this. The implicit support of industrial unionism should be re-examined in the light of the recent history of the British trade union movement.

Sectionalism

Hobsbawm argues that there is greater sectionalism in the labour movement than there was thirty years ago. This is questionable. There has always been sectionalism. We should reflect on the political success of the 1972 and '74 miners' strikes, the solidarity they engendered. Were they not more successful than the 1926 General Strike? This was the only occasion in the history of our movement where all trade unions fought together in taking strike action around support for the miners. It was in many respects a defeat. Hobsbawm gives credence perhaps to the 'myth of the golden past' notion: militancy and political consciousness have declined since the 1930s. This is highly contestable, bearing in mind the industrial dormancy of the 1930s in particular. Baldwin and the Tory government in 1926 won, Heath in 1974 lost.

Hobsbawm contends that the labour movement has stood still for thirty years—or not made substantial progress. True the full political potential of the very powerfully organized British trade union movement has yet to be demonstrated. Particular campaigning successes, important defensive victories, UCS for example, and Labour appearing to be the 'natural' party of government are all we can point to. However, the essential point is that British working people are more organized now than ever before. The potential of this fact is enormous and it is itself a major step forward. Certainly in the newer areas of trade union organization the political significance of trade unions is: (a) that democracy is a practice which has to be fought for and participated in—not something which is graciously provided by the ruling class; (b) it challenges the top-down way industry is run; (c) by its emphasis on activity and participation it challenges bourgeois ideology by weakening its basis of social support—trade unionism has an immanent radicalizing effect.

The Potential

Of course, in strictly electoral terms these effects are barely noticeable, and in the general political and social arenas little seems to have changed. My emphasis is on the potential. The necessity of the politically directed struggle of working people as the prime mover of fundamental change to capitalism is exactly the same as thirty years ago, and we seem as far away as ever. My argument is that potentialities are greater now. At least there is no readily mobilizable middle-ground mass of non-unionists that can be mobilized to support the capitalist class as there was in 1926.

One of the implications that can be drawn from Hobsbawm's thesis is that the organized labour movement is not as important as it was in the defining of a strategy for socialist transformation. It follows perhaps that students, women and cultural minorities assume a greater importance. This and the fashionable emphasis on ideological struggle needs to be rebuffed. The organized working class is central to our concept of a broad democratic alliance, and while struggle in all and every possible way against capitalism is essential, their orientation should always be towards the working class.

Mike Le Cornu

In his article Eric Hobsbawm states that the forward march of labour in this country, which Marx predicted, came to a halt several years ago. Was Marx's analysis correct at the time he made the prediction, or has some new element come into the situation which has caused the 'halt'? Hence the reason why I believe it is timely to engage in a Marxist analysis of the situation. Eric Hobsbawm, therefore, is to be congratulated for having initiated the discussion on this question and for the constructive manner in which he has conducted his argument. By contrast, the reaction to Eric Hobsbawm's article by Ken Gill, an influential comrade in the trade union movement, appears to lack that deep analytical content based on a scientific approach to the problem.

The fact that trade unions quite often embrace political objectives, albeit at times detrimental to their members' economic interests, is not proof of the political development of the trade union movement, as Ken Gill appears to claim. In fact I would suggest that political objectives expressed by trade union executive committees (and conferences in some cases) in resolutions, mean very little without the full knowledge and involvement of the membership in formulating them.

I believe we should face up to the possibility that it is the failure of our party and the left consciously to inject the necessary political content into the struggle which has largely contributed to the 'forward march of labour' having halted, though I agree with Kevin Halpin that to describe the movement as having 'halted' appears to be a negation of the Marxist concept of constant change.

It seems to me that many of our comrades adopt the all too simplistic view that the wage fight is the 'key' to everything, and many, including some who are trade union officials, apparently fail to realize or appreciate their own and the trade union and labour movement's (including our party's) contribution towards achieving the qualitative change in the situation which we are facing today.

Eric Hobsbawm, to my mind, correctly outlines the fact that today, because of the increase of workers in the public sector and the consequences of state monopoly capitalism, the effects of strikes are increasingly not directed at affecting the employers' profits, but at the amount of inconvenience to the public. This new phenomenon requires a political reappraisal as far as tactics and strategy are concerned in order to comply with the broad democratic alliance, which is a fundamental part of *The British Road to Socialism* and without which it will not be possible to achieve the necessary changes in policy towards our aim of establishing socialism.

The 'Key'

In my view it is an indication of political immaturity to single out any particular aspect of the class struggle as the 'key'. There are many keys in the struggle and only by applying a scientific approach to each aspect of the struggle will we know which key to use and when.

In spite of the fact that an increasing number of comrades see the need to fight for the alternative policy, it is still, by and large, a slogan. Many comrades are still blinded to real revolutionary activity by the militancy which a pure wage fight engenders, but which nevertheless remains part of the contradiction within capitalism. The wage struggle which took place in Ford's at the end of last year is a case in point. While the comrades employed in that particular enterprise can be commended for the role they played in assisting to develop the organization necessary to conduct such an overall dispute throughout the Ford complex, the tragedy is that the struggle emerged as an exercise of the market forces within the framework of capitalism.

In an interview conducted by the editor of *Marxism Today* in February 1979, Dan Connor, convenor of Ford's Body Plant at Dagenham, stated that the Ford workers' attitude towards the government's position on the 5 per cent was one where it was okay for those who work in other areas and don't make a profit, but unacceptable in relation to their position. The action of course provided a challenge to the Government's 5 per cent guideline, but are we not already aware of the development of state monopoly capitalism, so therefore it is inevitable that in that limited sense, wage fights will assume a political flavour. It is my view that this position should not be confused with the need to mobilize the workers at production level in a united manner along with the principles of the broad democratic alliance, confronting the Government with the alternative policy.

Economic Upsurge

When one surveys the past months' chaotic scene, one is aware that the wage settlement at Ford's (albeit in excess of the 5 per cent) has resulted in that large battalion of workers automatically becoming removed from and no longer a part of the 'army', challenging the government's drastic policy. Other sections of the workers, such as the lorry drivers, have progressively pulled out of the overall struggle as their respective wage settlements have been concluded. The struggle, which we have witnessed over the past months has, to my mind, been correctly described as 'the great economic upsurge'.

Unless we are able to show concrete evidence of a political advance or the raising of the political level of the workers engaged in struggle, we would do just as well to accept the Government guidelines. In my opinion failure to show this advance means that our actions are akin to running on a treadmill.

What I believe we should all be aware of is that struggle of any kind, unless deeply imbued with politics, can in fact result in prolonging the system which we seek to replace. Whatever gains are made simply get taken away by higher prices or by the introduction of tighter monetarist policies. This breeds disillusionment and despair and makes it more difficult to instill the necessary confidence in the fight for the alternative.

The Social Contract

Ken Gill disdainfully refers to the Social Contract as a 'political bargain', and later refers to the naïveté of trade union leaders expecting a Labour cabinet to fulfil its social commitments. It is a fact, of course, that the right wing seized the opportunity to manipulate the Social Contract into an instrument for unadulterated wage restraint which was subsequently unacceptable to the movement as such.

The dismissal of this 'political bargain' in blanket form, however, may well indicate a lack of confidence on our part to fully come to terms with this new situation of the trade union leadership and a Labour cabinet coming to terms on the basis of a contract.

Was there perhaps a twinge of opportunism? Was it safer for us to ensure we were batting on the winning side, by focusing attention on the negative element of, and the manner in which, the Social Contract was operated?

Self-Criticism

A fundamental principle of Marxism is to be self-critical. Perhaps at this late stage we can adopt a self-critical posture and seriously examine whether there was a failure on our part to apply a creative Marxist analysis to the new situation. We may well conclude that our party and the left in the labour movement should have been united in mobilizing the rank and file to mount the greatest possible pressure to ensure that the politically progressive demands contained in the Social Contract were carried out by the Labour Government.

Of course it would have required a massive challenge to the system, as Ken Gill quite correctly states, but isn't that precisely what we intend to do? It is my view that failure to mobilize the movement in this way, and for the purpose outlined, might well be costing us another dose of Toryism. There is no doubt in my mind that we should do everything possible to retain even a right-wing Labour government, and continue to strive for the alternative policy. This is only possible by involving the workers in every arena at grass root level, in the political fight for change.

As far as industrial workers are concerned, this must be done at shop floor level, taking up recognized issues in the respective areas, fighting for alternative policies at plant level, involving workers in the fight for industrial democracy at all levels and ensuring that they are fully aware of its implications. Our party and the left must ensure that the workers are aware of the importance of the public sector in the fight for socialism and therefore the need for its extension throughout industry. While the movement may have slowed down, I don't believe it has got stuck. It is we who, in my opinion, have failed to correctly analyse and give a clear lead. Perhaps one reason could be that our party too is tainted with the historical traditions of the British labour movement.

However, it is now that we must retrieve the situation. We are the only revolutionary party in Britain: we have a first class programme. Let us ensure that we follow the principles contained within it and that we play our role in transforming the present decadent system into socialism and a better life for all.

Royden Harrison

Thank you for inviting me to comment on the Marx Memorial Lecture delivered by my old friend and teacher, Eric Hobsbawm. On this occasion the master craftsman seems to have got it seriously 'out of true'. He concludes that during the last twenty-five or thirty years the long march of labour has been halted. Tragically this has happened just as British capitalist society has entered upon a crisis which is 'almost' a 'breakdown'.

My conclusion is very different: *since the end of the Second World War the British working class—without itself exhibiting the will to power—has established that it cannot be governed in the old way. It is not a footsore spectator at a crisis: it is that crisis.* The distinctive feature of the period is not the decline of the Labour vote, but the advent of majority Labour governments or the unprecedented striking down of those Tory ones which refuse to accept the terms of the new social settlement that was negotiated at the end of the war: an end to the reserve army of labour: comprehensive social services: the mixed economy.

With sincere respect: Eric Hobsbawm delivered a Marx Memorial *service* rather than a Lecture. Once you start writing about 'marches' rather than 'struggles' you put yourself in the tradition of Francis Williams rather than of Karl Marx. And you end up writing the sequel to *Magnificent Journey—Inconsequential Jog!*

In Favour of Eric the Red

The best cure for the depression induced by the new Hobsbawm

(Eric or Little by Less) is to consult the spirit and immaculate standards of the Old Eric (Eric the Red). He has not left us. He has merely had an off day.

Among Hobsbawm's most enviable strengths as an historian is his sure eye for turning points and his confident marking of our chronology. Yet in this lecture he takes for his starting post some uncertain and seemingly arbitrary date between 1949 and 1954. If he had chosen 1945 he would have preferred the more obvious and the better vantage point. After all, when one reads contemporary history by a great historian one expects to recover one's own experience at a deeper level. And just as Eric fails to remind me of where I was when we 'sprang' the Pentonville Five or marched on a place called Saltley, so his chronology prevents me from re-living the moment when the polls were declared in the summer after the end of the war in Europe when we ushered in not only the heroic years of British social democracy, but the habit of Labour government. Between 1886 and 1945 the Conservatives were in office for 75 per cent of the time and—with only a very slight extravagance—it has been said that when they were not in office they were still in power.

From 1945 they have been in office for barely 50 per cent of the time and then they were not in power: not in the old way. They either respected the new social settlement or else the workers rose against them and chucked them out. It was the great limitation of 'Super Mac' that he presided over 'Butskellism': he restored the semblance of political tradition at the expense of a marked relative decline in the strength of the British capitalist economy. The most accomplished British prime minister since the war was brought low; not by a prostate or by a Profumo; but by his final inability to reconcile the requirements of his party with the necessities of his class. The unsettled character of the new social settlement was finally exposed when, by the failing light of the new technology, the British workman could still be discerned answering the foreman back. His answer may well be pedestrian—I have no doubt that it is vulgar—but it poses the question: which is it to be—socialism, or the ruin of the two contending classes? (There is a third possibility. But that requires us to think of Sir Keith Joseph in the role of the 'Chicago Boys' and Mrs Thatcher in the part of General Pinochet. At the same time of writing we have not come to that nor is it a denouement which I find easily imaginable even though some of my best friends are looking forward to that catastrophe: on the understanding, of course, that it will assume an agreeable English form.)

Quantity before Quality: Obscuring Events Behind Trends

Of late, Eric has become a great man for statistics. His lecture is largely given over to counting the declining Labour vote and the stationary population of trade unionists and the declining proportion of the occupied to be found in the manual working class and the growing number of women in paid employment. God forbid that I should be thought to be an opponent of quantitative methods—I will never receive another grant from the Social Science Research Council if that misapprehension becomes current! Social history is nothing if it is not about numbers: only, please to remember it is not about history if it is not about *unique events*. I like my conclusions to be accurate: and the last word in accuracy is not a word but a number. But the trouble is that one has never in history or politics had the 'last word' when one tries to put it into that conclusive shape.

My purpose is not to call into question the interest or the reliability of Eric's statistics. Indeed, I am happy to reinforce them for him. If he had looked at individual Labour Party *membership*, as well as support, he would have found that it declined by a quarter of a million between 1951 and 1970. Yet the statistics to which he attends are less important than the ones to which I attend. Nor is this a purely subjective judgement. The incidence of majority Labour governments may help to explain declining Labour support and membership whereas the argument can certainly not be made to work the other way round. It is only when we take the two statistical series together that they point to the heart of our experience: the profoundly equivocal nature of Labour government.

About the equivocal nature of these governments Eric has

nothing whatsoever to say. One way of reading the statistics that he sets before us would be to maintain that the working class, if it has not seen through the sham, has been so disspirited by it that it has concluded that the distribution of wealth and power in favour of the capitalists and their hangers-on is irreversible. This position is available, but it cannot be securely occupied unless one can maintain that it is more significant than the progress which has been made within the party by the Labour left.

Now Eric has always had a rather poor opinion of the Labour left. He has always been inclined to treat it as if it was negligible. There was considerable justification for that attitude up until about 1959. But in that year the defeat of Gaitskell at the Blackpool Conference and the formation of the Campaign for Democratic Socialism signalled the beginning of the descent of the right wing into a faction. One really invites the charge of displaying a kind of petulant sectarianism if one totally ignores the way in which at party conference, on the NEC and in an increasing number of constituency parties the Labour right has come to feel that it is on the defensive and at risk. Those who in earlier periods thought of themselves as the natural and inevitable leaders of the party huddle together in their precarious majority within the PLP and discuss their chances in relation to that slow—but highly civilized—purge of opportunists and careerists which has been, and which is, proceeding. Nor will it do to pretend that the passing of the leadership of this left from Michael Foot to Tony Benn is but the last episode in the squalid annals of Labour's lost leaders: men who have assumed the mantle of the left while they were waiting in the wings, only to discard it the moment they were on the centre of the stage. It is not merely that Benn has courageously acknowledged the place of the Marxists within the party; it is that he has conducted himself differently from his predecessors and identified himself with politics —which are *not merely electoral*. This stance has an historical importance which exists whether Benn himself maintains it or abandons it.

The Unions and the Transformation of the Wages Question

Just as Eric finds the big fact about the Labour Party to be the decline in its electoral support, so he finds the big facts about trade unionism to be the relative stagnation in trade union membership and the growth of sectionalism. The astonishing growth of white-collar unionism is allowed as some small and seemingly dubious consolation. The prodigious growth of unionism among women workers (from 31 per cent in 1974 to 36.6 per cent in 1978) is not mentioned. The labour unrest of 1970-74 is passed over in a few lines despite the fact that it quite dwarfed its predecessor of 1910-14 in terms of its daring, its comprehensiveness and its success. Where was Eric during those mass strikes some of which turned not on the conditions of production (wages and hours) but on the condition of distribution (pay beds and gun boats for Chile)? What was he doing during the hundreds of factory occupations when the assertion of the right to work reduced the rights of property to silence? What was he up to during the civil disobedience that followed the passing of the Industrial Relations Act and the Housing Finance Act. What stage had he reached on his long march when the miners revenged 1926 and went on to lead the entire movement into the struggle that ended in the fall of the Tory Government?

Was he contemplating 'the growth of sectionalism'? Now this is the part of his lecture that I find most difficult to comprehend. I entirely agree with him when he insists that increasing industrial militancy does not lead on in some simple or necessary way to socialist consciousness. I understood him when he points out that under the conditions of state monopoly capitalism the consequences of sectionalism are likely to become more disagreeable and perhaps more divisive. But if the consequences are greater that does not mean that the thing itself has become more pronounced.

Eric hardly needs me to remind him that sectionalism is one of the oldest traditions of the British trade union movement. Even in the heady days of Owenite general unionism there were still the 'Pukes' and the 'Exclusives'. I rather fancy that he and I might agree that some of our fellow Labour historians have been a little too quick to identify the non-wage issues that lurk behind 'higher' forms of action and sometimes a bit slow on the uptake when it comes to detecting the sectional interests that can be concealed within solidarity or other 'approved' issues. But a growth in sectionalism is difficult to accept in a period in which the *number of trade unionists* has been rising and the *number of unions falling*. In particular it is a bit difficult to reconcile with a period which has for one of its distinctive characteristics, the habitual recourse to—and acceptance of—incomes policies.

I quite accept that capitalism has always had an incomes policy in the sense that the aim of its controllers has always been to keep wages as low as possible. But it seems to be a distinctive feature of our period—except for time of war—that it is driven to pursue this end through formal agreements which it seeks to impose upon the entire movement whether by negotiation or directly by statute. On balance, these policies have been rather successful from the capitalist point of view since they have been associated with a slackening in the growth of real wages or else, as in the case of the Social Contract, with quite pronounced reductions in them. Trade unionists—the led as well as the leaders—have repeatedly accepted this burden as a duty which they owe the Commonwealth. One may hold—with Arthur Scargill—that they have been deluded in behaving in this manner; that they have fallen victims to the 'Social Contrick'; but to reproach them with exhibiting a 'growth of sectionalism' is merely to add insult to injury.

For my part, while I take as glum a view as the next man about most of the practical consequences of these exercises in incomes policy, I not only find in them a distinctive feature of our period, but in their *principle* a possible future. More than a hundred years ago Marx complained that in the traditional and habitual modes of their action, the trade unions dealt with *effects* rather than with the *causes* from which those effects proceeded. He made no clear suggestions as to how this limitation was to be surmounted and so far as Eric Hobsbawm merely protests against the traditional preoccupation with the 'wages question' to the exclusion of more important matters he does not either. But in our time the wages question is being transformed under our eyes from a *sectional* into a *class* question, from an *industrial* one into a *political* one. This has become agenda. The capitalist must go—top hat in hand—to negotiate with the TUC about the appropriate rate of extraction of surplus value. Slowly—very slowly—the trade unions have been coming to insist that everything should be made negotiable. The more farsighted members of the bourgeoisie have been coming to see that *that* would definitely not be 'constitutional'!

Where Have All the Marxists Gone?

Thus, the working people, poor bone-headed slouches that they are, have ignored the directions that we gave them and the routes that we prescribed for them. They may have fallen out of the long march, but have they stumbled on to the field of battle. And in the confusion of the battle, and despite many self-inflicted wounds, one thing is becoming increasingly clear: they are not to be easily defeated. For victory they only require a belief in themselves and a Clausewitz to supply, not a preconceived strategy, but the one appropriate to the surrounding terrain and the prevailing disposition of forces.

Why have the 'cadres' gone absent without leave? Perhaps the strangest feature of Eric's lecture is that it almost completely neglects the discussion of 'the vanguard' and it wholly neglects the task of locating the whereabouts of the British labour movement in terms of international developments. Of these two omissions, the second is the more extraordinary. One of the most conspicuous features of his career as a Marxist historian has been the way in which Hobsbawm has supplied an uncompromising challenge to the insularity that still distinguishes the work of most of the rest of us. Yet we would surely need to believe—as I do not believe—that the history and the role of the British Communist Party is entirely unimportant before an assessment of this period could avoid any reference to events in Moscow or in Budapest or in Prague, or to their repercussions upon it. It amounts to a radical form of 'inauthenticity'. It is as if the *traison des clercs* was to be seen upside down as in a camera obscura.

The tragedy of our time is not, as Eric seems to suppose, that the British working class has been playing the spectator at its own funeral. The tragedy is rather that Marxism has become an ideology in the strict Marxist sense of the term. It has become the necessarily false consciousness of the industrial revolution of the twentieth century: a revolution which has to be brought about upon the basis of an international transfer of an achieved technology and under the conditions of imperialism. Marxism is at once the subject of that irony and the only intellectual resource capable of disclosing it.

The English working class is in need of its Marxists. May Eric Hobsbawm, with his great learning and his wonderful analytical intelligence, help to restore them to us.

Stan Newens

Eric Hobsbawm pinpoints a number of symptoms of the stagnation of the socialist movement in Britain at the present time, which are extremely unpalatable to the left. In his contribution, Ken Gill does not attempt to deny these—that Britain has slipped behind other countries in the percentage of workers organized in trade unions, that the Labour (plus Communist) vote has fallen back and that the number of socialist activists—particularly manual workers—has declined.

He prefers to ignore them and merely asserts that the development of a militant wages movement is the first priority. In so doing, as Peter Carter comments in his article he appears to be arguing that fighting for wages will eventually bring down capitalism—a doubtful proposition. The idea that socialism can be built on such a basis is even more dubious.

Wage Militancy

If wage militancy were a measure of socialist drive, some American trade unions would be leading the vanguard. However, as they regularly demonstrate, it is perfectly possible to combine the toughest trade union bargaining methods with a wholehearted commitment to capitalism.

Although Ken Gill argues that wage struggles in the era of state monopoly capitalism are no longer pure wage struggles, this is certainly what they are in the eyes of the majority of the participants. Far from believing that society is in need of radical reorganization, they believe it is a question of forcing employers to pay up, and they join up to advance their own sectional interests.

In fact, wage militancy frequently goes hand-in-hand with a belief in the fundamental viability of the system. Insofar as socialists argue, like Kevin Halpin, that industry is tremendously profitable, it follows that striking for more pay is all that is required to improve living standards. Political action is subordinate to this and of marginal importance only.

It is only when it becomes part of the consciousness of large numbers of workers and their families that enterprises are unable to survive, and that the system as a whole is incapable of resolving these problems, that political activity in favour of root and branch change can be generated on a broad front. In 1945, there was a mass conviction, based upon years of mass experience with Tory or near-Tory governments at the helm, that only the political action to which the Labour Party was pledged would prevent a return to the stagnation and unemployment of the 1930s.

The experience of the last generation has been very different. With all its faults, the welfare state provides a safety net for the elderly, the unemployed, the sick and most who fall upon difficult times, which did not exist in pre-war days. A Labour government has been in power more than the Conservatives in recent years and, along with all its caution, equivocation and reliance on bureaucracy, has been identified at least by many younger people with the establishment. It has been possible for whole sections of the workforce to achieve improvements in living standards through trade union activity pure and simple. The fact that a Labour government has frequently been under attack from the left as well as the Conservatives has helped to spread the impression that the issues are trivial and personal.

This was reflected in the recent General Election in which Labour sustained a catastrophic defeat in southern England. The grown-up children of solid Labour parents voted Conservative in huge numbers in the suburbs, the outer metropolitan areas, new towns and overspill areas. They have come to accept the basic values and ideology of a capitalist society and have no consciousness of the need for fundamental change.

Capitalism in Crisis

Yet capitalism is in very deep crisis. Far from making huge profits, many key enterprises would have collapsed but for huge state subsidies. This is true in steel, shipbuilding, motor cars, machine tools, and a myriad of enterprises dependent on them. The fundamental basis of the capitalist crisis is the decline in the rate of profit and this is manifest in the economic crisis of the moment.

The argument of socialists should not therefore be based on the contention that every demand can be met from profits or from some source related to it, which may convince at Ford but will not at Leyland. The case for socialism rests on the proposition that the contradictions of capitalism will eventually cause it to fail and grind to a halt.

This is what is happening before our very eyes. Industries are failing and Britain is being de-industrialized. Owing to the relative scarcity of certain raw materials, but above all oil and energy, capitalist booms of the old variety can never really get started before they produce enormous inflationary pressures, which are nothing to do with wage increases, but reflect rising oil prices. Increasingly, the governments of capitalist countries are co-operating to achieve anti-inflationary, that is essentially low growth, policies.

A Socialist Alternative

Socialists ought therefore to be emphasizing the alternatives to the stagnation and chronic crisis of contemporary capitalism and advancing programmes designed to achieve them. Trade unionists—particularly those in the white-collar and public sector who have only comparatively recently been recruited on the basis of defending their own sectional interests—must be won over to supporting these programmes.

The relevance of the extension of social ownership (for example to banks and financial institutions even for those employed in them), economic planning, opening the books, industrial democracy and control over what is produced needs to be driven home. Similarly, the desirability of providing aid and credit to developing countries on a generous scale not only in the interests of international solidarity but to enlarge employment opportunities at home, ought to be argued.

There is even at the present time a certain amount of groundswell among shop stewards, environmentally-orientated groups and others which indicates that such ideas are being generated independently. Unfortunately, socialists are not always backing this—not to speak of the official trade union movement, whose half-hearted response to the Lucas Aerospace shop stewards' plan and other similar initiatives is typical.

Dangers of Sectionalism

It would, of course, be wrong to suggest that the setback to labour's forward march is merely the result of failing to advance the right policies. Objective conditions over which we have very little control fundamentally determine mass consciousness. If, however, as seems inevitable, the crisis of the capitalist system continues and deepens, its credibility will be increasingly undermined and people will become more receptive to alternative ideas. In such circumstances, the advocacy and application of relevant programmes can greatly accelerate the change of consciousness necessary for moving forward towards a socialist goal.

If, however, we blandly assume that all that is required is to fight the class struggle in terms of wages and conditions and at some unspecified future date, in some unspecified and unfathomed way, organized labour will turn to socialism, we may well find that sectionalism will gain ground, racialism may flourish and catastrophic disasters may ensue.

Ken Gill's argument that the movement's forward march is marked by the replacement of the Deakins and Lawthers by the Joneses and the Scanlons has already been overtaken by the replacement of the Scanlons by the Duffys—a development which may yet produce dramatic setbacks in the higher councils of the TUC and the Labour Party.

The return of a Conservative government under Mrs Thatcher, whatever its effects in galvanizing the labour movement into a new burst of activity, must be seen as an expression of the failure of the left. It is not enough to assume that revulsion at the effects of her policies will automatically carry us forward anew. The painful truths in Eric Hobsbawm's article will remain.

If the left can formulate and advocate the relevant political strategy, however, we shall be in a much better position to take advantage of any new impetus. Such a strategy must rule out proposals for accepting capitalism. We need to face up to the problems of world poverty, the destruction of the environment, the exhaustion of resources, the energy crisis and the dangers of world war and show that these can only be tackled by radical steps involving drastic cuts in arms, the extension of social ownership, real economic planning designed to produce for need not just profit, the introduction of genuine industrial and political democracy, increased overseas aid et cetera. Proposals to achieve these can be linked to the ordinary day-to-day needs and aspirations of the British people and provide a comprehensive alternative to the increasingly crisis-ridden conditions of our times.

Only on such a basis will labour's forward march be resumed with any real hope of building a socialist society.

Response

Eric Hobsbawm

Since the very lively and serious discussion on 'the forward march of labour halted?' was started a year ago, it seems reasonable that the author of the original article should now comment on the debate. I hope this will not be misunderstood as trying to have the last word. The discussion must and will go on. The questions it has raised are too important to be put on the shelf and, since the bitter experience of the last election, it is clearer than ever that the British labour movement has not yet found satisfactory answers to them. Nor is this second intervention intended to exaggerate the significance of the first article. This was originally given early in 1978 as a Marx Memorial Lecture, and it was not intended as a political statement (except insofar as all Marxists try to unite theory and practice), but as a historian's survey of what had happened to the British working class over the past century. There would have been no discussion at all, if people in the movement, and above all people with active responsibilities as union officials or shop stewards, had not recognized that important and urgent questions for our movement emerged from this survey and had not taken them up.

The 1979 Election

What is at issue is not whether the forward march of labour has been halted in some respects, but whether this retreat is offset, or more than offset, by other developments in the British labour movement. About the halt there can, unfortunately, be no doubt. Some indications about the falling electoral support for the Labour Party, its declining membership, and the comparative stagnation of trade union membership were given in the original article. They could have been supplemented by data about the declining support of trade unionists for the Labour Party, as indicated by the payment of the political levy. The general election of 1979 has unfortunately confirmed this analysis.

To put the matter briefly. Labour polled fewer votes than at any time since 1931, nor did any significant number of these lost votes go to other candidates of the socialist or communist left. Labour only barely exceeded the Conservatives among the skilled working-class voters. Somthing like a third of *trade unionists* appear actually to have voted for the Tories. Since 1974 the swing to the Conservatives among trade unionists seems to have been something like 7 per cent, among unskilled workers 6.5 per cent, among skilled workers no less than 11 per cent. Almost 10 per cent of first-time voters swung right, compared to 1974. These disastrous developments are not offset by the good showing of Labour in Scotland, by the immigrant vote, by the resistance of women to the appeal of the Tories (their swing was only 3 per cent compared to 9.5 per cent among the men), and by the interesting fact that the Labour vote actually rose significantly among the smallish professional and managerial group. (These data are taken from public opinion polls, but there is no reason to think that they are not roughly correct.) What makes these results even more disappointing is, that the percentage of voters actually rose a little. People who had not bothered to vote previously went to the polls—and they chose the Tories. In short, there is no comfort to be got from the 1979 election.

Positive Developments

As against these negative trends, several contributors, starting with Ken Gill, have drawn attention to positive developments. First, and in the most general sense, the British working class 'without itself exhibiting the will to power, has established that it cannot be governed in the old way' (Royden Harrison). This is clearly a fundamentally new factor in British politics since the war and, insofar as British capitalism is unable—or unable any longer—to meet its demands, in the British economy. Second, and more specifically, there is the rising tide of militancy and industrial struggle, which reached a peak in 1970–74, but has continued or resumed at a high level. Third, there is the political power of this militancy as demonstrated by the role of the TUC in politics and by the fall of the Heath Government in 1974; people on the left are less inclined to cite the difficulties it caused the Labour Government in 1978–9. Fourth, it is argued that this militancy has led to a shift to the left in the leadership of the trade union movement accompanied by a shift to the left within the Labour Party—even by the virtual abdication of the old Jenkinsite right wing, within the parliamentary Labour Party. Fifth—the point has once again been made by Royden Harrison—there is the emergence of a new and politically more promising Labour left as typified by Benn.

In practice therefore the case for an advance of labour rests essentially on the industrial movement, in recent years overwhelmingly a wages movement, and this is recognized in the discussion, which has dealt mainly with the character, possibilities and limitations of trade union action. I do not want to discuss the political shift within the Labour Party and elsewhere on the left in detail. There has been an undoubted and welcome advance here. Most of the old Labour right has indeed been pushed out of the Labour Party or out of politics. Tony Benn's Labour left, unlike its predecessors for a very long time, actually has a policy, including a policy for tackling the economic problems of Britain. It is indeed the only such policy on offer from within a major party, other than Mrs Thatcher's and Sir Keith Joseph's proposal to turn the economic clock back to about 1865. The possibilities of united action by socialists and communists are indeed better than they have been for many years, the chief obstacle being probably the sectarianism of some smaller groups on the unfortunately fragmented left. But at present these welcome developments represent what is happening within a badly defeated Labour Party, whose active

membership is dangerously small—perhaps not more than
300,000 people—and not necessarily representative of its mass
support; and a Communist Party and other groups on the left
which are, to put it mildly, not growing. Moreover, with the
recent shift to the right in the leadership of some unions which,
as Stan Newens pointed out 'may yet produce dramatic setbacks
in the higher councils of the TUC and the Labour Party', it is too
early to start counting chickens. It is certainly wrong to
overlook the prospects of a future advance, but they are in an as
yet uncertain future.

Power of Trade Union Movement

On the other hand the trade union movement is powerful,
effective and in recent years highly militant, and evidently
changing and developing fast. Nor can it be denied that it has a
powerful rank-and-file base. Indeed, the shift of the unions'
centre of gravity from official structure to plant and shop floor is
characteristic of the past twenty years—and until recently it
has accelerated. The contrast between the weakness of the
political side of the movement and the power and dynamism of
the industrial side has been striking. It is natural that the left has
been tempted to overrate the possibilities and underrate the
limits of purely industrial action. There has been precious little
else to cheer about.

Its achievements, particularly in the years 1969–74, have
indeed been striking, and contributors to the discussion have
been right to criticize me for not saying enough about them. It is
probably true, as Steve Jeffreys of the Socialist Workers Party
has argued, that it has ensured the survival of the strong
traditional kind of working-class consciousness (limited though
this was and is) in spite of the decline of the old nineteenth-
century industries which provided its main base and the
numerical decline of the old (male) skilled worker who played
such a crucial role in it; and in spite of the great improvement in
standards of living which middle class observers in the 1950s
expected to lead to 'bourgeoisification'. It has made it possible

to integrate the rapidly growing non-manual and white-collar workers into the labour movement and thereby to some extent into the working class. Though something like 40 per cent of unionists are today white-collar workers this has not led to a lowering of militancy. Today it is not only the traditional manual worker who practises union solidarity and refuses to cross picket lines. It has made it easier to integrate the enormously increased number of (often part-time) working women in the organized labour movement. And it made possible the victories of 1969–74.

The Limits of This Consciousness

And yet the limits of this renovated 'trade union consciousness' have not been overcome. They have even been emphasized by the concurrent decline in the *political* class movement. It has been argued that trade union action has not been divorced from politics, because it has also conducted non-economist struggles (such as that over pay beds in hospitals) and because left-wing unions and activists take political stands. This is true to some extent, though the overwhelming majority of political strikes in recent years have actually been on economic issues, directly or indirectly against government attempts to limit free bargaining and to cut down union rights. It has also been argued that they are political in the sense that they will in some unspecified way regenerate the political movement, broaden mass support for a socialist policy and unify the working people of the country. There is not so far much evidence for this.

It is not enough to say that 'in our time the "wages question" is being transformed under our eyes from a *sectional* into a *class* question; from an *industrial* one into a *political* one' (Royden Harrison). This has long been so; capitalists and governments have acted on this assumption. But there is an enormous difference between periods when the wage question in this form is part of a wider political upsurge of the working class, as between 1918 and the General strike (the Labour vote rose from about two to about eight millions between 1918 and 1929), and periods like the present, when this is not the case. In short, trade unionism alone is not enough, as Marxists have argued, ever since Karl Marx himself, against syndicalists and others of their kind. And the present phase of militancy is overwhelmingly trade unionist and economistic, mainly on the issue of wages. There is no real disagreement about this. What is unclear is 'the type of relation which exists between wages and the political struggle' (Pete Carter), and how the wages struggle is to be integrated into the wider struggle of which it is only one part. I believe that this is the crucial problem which faces the labour movement today.

For of course—as Roger Murray rightly reminds us—'the wages struggle will go on, regardless. . . . I think the denunciation of wages struggles as economistic . . . while being accurate in some ways, is unhelpful'. This needs to be said. It would be a curious kind of labour movement that paid no attention to what working people are actually fighting for—to what in crisis and inflation they are almost bound to fight for. But of course there is no danger of that. The danger lies rather in rationalizing militant economism into a general strategy.

Sectionalism

Its limitations have been brought out in the discussion, not least by some of those active on the industrial front. There is sectionalism. 'The wages struggle in *isolation* and conducted *sectionally* can and does divide the labour movement, isolate it from other sections and assist the right-wing drift' (Roger Murray). Whether sectionalism is stronger in the trade union movement today than in the past, as I suggested, is an historical question on which I may well have been wrong. It is not worth discussing here. The fact remains that sectionalism—of a different kind from the past perhaps—exists *today*, and that (in Royden Harrison's words) 'under the conditions of state and monopoly capitalism the consequences of sectionalism are likely to become more disagreeable and more divisive'. We all know this, not least the comrades active in industry.

There is also the tendency of 'straight' trade unionism to take the capitalist system as given and to concentrate on getting the best terms within it. This has always been the weakness of the British trade union movement, 'an opposition which never becomes the government' as R.H. Tawney pointed out long ago, and of the characteristic 'trade-unionist' form of British working-class consciousness which has prevented it from 'exhibiting the will to power' (Royden Harrison). It can easily lead to integrating itself into capitalism. At least one major strike of 1978 has been described in the discussion as 'an exercise of the market forces within the framework of capitalism' (Mike Le Cornu). There are great dangers here. The call for the abolition on all restraints on free wage-bargaining may at times be a crucial slogan, but we might remember that the call for the abolition of restraints on the free operations of the market (of which it is a special form) usually has very different political implications.

Trade Union Action and Political Consciousness

There is, thirdly, the fact that trade union action—even militant action—can be quite divorced from political consciousness. The dockers who struck in solidarity with their imprisoned comrades in 1972 were the same men who had protested against Heath's sacking of Enoch Powell and who jeered Bernadette Devlin outside Pentonville Jail. The fact that over a third of trade unionists voted Tory in 1979, many of them no doubt participants in industrial action, is a sad reminder of this. All the more when we remember that there was a time when trade union membership or background and voting for Labour used to go together.

We may therefore conclude that trade union power and militancy alone important though they are, have not offset, *and by themselves* cannot offset, the setbacks of the labour movement in other respects.

The Next Stage of the Debate

But what can be done about it? This must clearly be the subject of the next stage of the debate. The discussion so far has brought forward a number of general suggestions and some more specific proposals, mainly about how to link the industrial struggle with wider demands and struggles, but I don't think anyone believes that satisfactory answers have been found. They cannot be found by wishing the British working class and its movement different from what it has historically been and become. They cannot be found by concentrating on its most advanced sections—whether the active members of the Labour and Communist parties or other parties and groups. The test of vanguards lies in their ability to lead armies. They cannot be found by concentrating on one aspect of the fight of labour—the industrial struggle, which has naturally formed a large part of the discussion—even if this is at present the nearest thing to a mass mobilization of the working people. There are, after all, today something like 350,000 shop stewards. They cannot be found by adding up various sections of the population who, for one reason or another, may find the left supporting their sectional demands.

Forward Again

A class party of labour (with all its limitations) became the mass party of the British working class (or, since we are a multinational state, the British working classes) by giving unity to the class consciousness of this class as a whole, and offering, in addition to the defence of material or other special interests, confidence, self-respect and hope of a different and better society. How did this come about? Why did millions of workers and others after 1918 and again during and after the Second World War, turn to Labour? Why have, even today, certain groups—the Scots, women, a modest but growing section of the middle classes—in varying degrees resisted the turn towards toryism? These questions have not been adequately analysed and studied by the left. Perhaps such study may help our movement to find its way forward again. The discussion in *Marxism Today* and elsewhere is welcome because it recognizes a serious crisis in the development of the movement. But there is no reason to believe that the faltering of Labour as a political mass movement is historically inevitable or cannot be reversed.

2

Tony Benn

an interview with Eric Hobsbawm

Let me begin by saying that those of us who have been around a long time tend to have a sense of déja vu. We are back again in a period of a major crisis of world capitalism, combined with a very dangerous international situation, and this is, of course, the general setting within which the specific and very grave problems of Great Britain, the British economy and British politics are being played out. The first thing I'd like to ask you is, how do you see this present crisis? How would you compare it with the last time around?

I too am struck by the similarities between the situation now and that in the 1930s, in that, as far as this country is concerned, we are locked into a virtual collapse of our industry which has proceeded more rapidly than people expected and which has been coming for some time. The decline is beginning at a lower level of activity than we had in the 1930s, and forms part of a world capitalist crisis which is at the moment also deepening, with very severe unemployment in the United States and in the EEC.

It looks at the moment as if the Government, far from trying to revive the British economy, is using this crisis in order to secure certain very clear political objectives. Namely, if possible, the destruction of trade union power in the land by three processes: by stimulating unemployment to frighten working people away from trade unionism; by legislation to make effective trade unionism very difficult, if not impossible; and by the utilization of the media in a very sustained campaign to persuade the

British public that the trade union movement is responsible for our problems and has got to be weakened if we are to recover from them. It would also be true to say that in this slump we have a government that no longer has a patriotic element in its capitalism and actually sees a future for the people they represent in the success of international capitalism even at the expense of the UK's becoming a sort of Northern Ireland of the Common Market.

On the other hand, the trade union movement is much stronger than it was in the 1930s, in terms of numbers. Also, a lot of people are clearer in their own mind about what is happening. The option of war as a solution to the problem of the slump has been rendered absurd, though not impossible, because of the development of nuclear weapons, and I think these factors make the situation slightly different.

One point on which I would like to push you a little further: it seems to me that this crisis, both in the world as a whole and in Britain, is also to some extent a crisis of the political and social structures that have grown up during the period of capitalist expansion, in the long and short term. During the last crisis this took the form of fascism. In the present crisis it probably does not. But is there an analogy? An analogous expression of difficulties, tensions, breakdowns in the traditional political and social structures of the old established Western countries and particularly Britain?

Yes I think there is. But this problem is not confined to the Western world. One could argue that the industrial development of technology as it has been applied, particularly military technology, has centralized power in both Eastern and Western societies, and that if we are talking about the crisis of political structures we must also include the crisis of bureaucratization in the Soviet Union and Eastern Europe. I think one could reasonably argue that in no major country in the world is the government absolutely certain that it carries the consent of its own people. For as society becomes more interconnected and hence more vulnerable, the pressure for central power and central control gets stronger. To this extent I would argue that a democratic socialist challenge would be a challenge to all existing power structures, both in Eastern Europe and in Western Europe. And to the extent that the state has become bureaucratized, the trade unions have become incorporated in a declining consensus that is becoming more authoritarian. Part of the crisis lies in the fact that people have lost their confidence in the power of the state to solve the problem in a way that would preserve their independence and their freedom and liberty.

There are in fact a number of parallel crises in train at the same time, and that is why I think we have to look at them not only in terms of socialist analysis, but also in terms of a direct, sustained democratic challenge everywhere in the world to the secretive exercise of centralized power working through bureaucracy. This is what gives an added dimension to the argument, in respect of both the development of capitalism and the development of communism.

You said that the trade union movement today is stronger than it was, say, in the 1930s. That may be so. But would you say that on the whole the socialist movement, the democratic movement, the people's movement, have shown themselves strong enough to mount an effective challenge, both to the crisis itself, and to the forces such as Thatcherism, which it has brought out?

If you mean 'Have we yet succeeded in building a winning coalition of people who understand what is happening and recognize the role of trade unionism and socialism in preventing the disaster from overwhelming us?' then no, clearly we have not. If you mean 'Is there a residual strength and a potential strength in the instruments of democracy, the instruments of trade unionism and the ideas of socialism, capable of being mobilized and developed to prevent this from reaching its ultimate form of repression?', I think the answer must be Yes. Otherwise I would be wholly pessimistic about the prospects.

We have seen twenty years of surrender. Since 1959, the parliamentary leadership of the Labour Party has been going along with the idea that the post-war consensus, built upon full employment and the welfare state, was a permanent feature of life in Britain and that trade unionism would be brought into a position where it helped to run it. That response has failed to command the support of our people because they have seen, first, that it did not contain within it any element whatsoever of transformation, and second, that even by its own criteria it failed. That policy could not bring about growth, it could not extend freedom, it could not even maintain, let alone develop, welfare, and it could not sustain full employment. The turning point came when, in 1976, the IMF simply dictated to a Labour government full of social democrats ordering them to abandon even social democracy. That was the background of failure, but the potential strength is still there. If I didn't believe that I would give up hope altogether, which I see no reason whatever to do.

You talked of residual and potential strength. Do you mean to say that you are thinking in terms of mobilizing forces that were mobilized once and can be mobilized again, or of discovering newer and wider forces that can be mobilized?

Both. If you look back at 1945, which was the first election that I was active in, although I did distribute labour literature ten years earlier, the amazing thing was the extent to which we were able to mobilize young and old, left and right, men and women, Scots, English and Welsh, the trade union members and the Labour Party. We mobilized a huge body of opinion in favour of a clear policy of reform. I know these were modest reforms by modern standards, amounting to little more than the final fruition of the radical ideas of the 1906 government, amplified by a bit of Fabianism, a bit of Churchill in his various Liberal-Conservative roles, and a bit of Macmillan with his *Middle Way*. But we mobilized a powerful combination committed to change. Unfortunately that spirit escaped and evaporated during the period of successive Labour governments after 1951.

May I stop you for a moment. You have talked about the 1945 government. In your Guildhall lecture[1] *you talked of Attlee's as a social and socialist revolution. Are you talking about the same thing?*

Yes – because there are two ways of looking at the 1945 government. One is to look at it in the way in which I tried to answer your question: is it possible to mobilize a wide range of people who will clearly support major change? Secondly, did the 1945 government achieve a real social revolution? The answer to that is that at the time, and compared to the slump of earlier years, in terms of what it was able to achieve, it did. But when you analyse it with the benefit of hindsight, you can see that it was also in a sense the final fruition of a liberal and radical tradition: though that isn't to say it wasn't a very significant turning point for Britain in the mid century because it was. But it would not be adequate to go back to 1945 policies now and argue that they would suffice for the next time round, because the nature of the crisis we shall inherit, whenever we win the next election, will in many ways be much more fundamental than that which Attlee had to face in 1945. For our industry will have been destroyed, we will have a lot of long-term unemployed, and the economy will be in a much much weaker state than it was even in 1945.

But surely we can't go back to 1945. I mean 1945 was, as it were, an earlier moment in the development of the labour and democratic movement. One of the things that has often struck me, perhaps it has also struck you, is that the curve of Labour Party support starts in 1900 and goes on, with a slight interruption in 1931, up to 1951 with the Labour Party becoming increasingly not merely the party of the working class, but also to some extent the inheritor of a wide popular coalition including the other nationalities of this country, intellectuals, the workers and others. This went on until the early fifties, and from then on it seems to me there has been a gradual erosion and the problem for us is how we can halt and

---

[1] The Granada Guildhall Lecture on Trade Unions given by Tony Benn on May 15 1980.

reverse this erosion. There was a brief moment in the middle sixties when it looked as though the tendency was going to be reversed. It hasn't yet been. The erosion has continued. And to call for a return to 1945 seems hardly adequate.

I am not saying we should. I was trying to answer your question—is it possible to mobilize wide and residual forces and new forces?—and I said it had been done in 1945 for a programme that was appropriate for that period. That task has been achieved once and can be achieved again. The policies to which we will have to attach support next time will be much more radical because events will require them to be much more radical than they were in 1945. But don't romanticize the thirties. In 1935 there were three million unemployed, yet only 150 Labour MPs were elected to Parliament. To suppose that there was a steady rise in support during the thirties and that 1945 was inevitable in terms of the public response we received would be to romanticize it. As you know, in 1945 Herbert Morrison did not even want all that public ownership, and it was an amendment moved at the annual conference by Ian Mikardo that eventually led to the wide extension of public ownership. We must be very clear that even in 1945 there were people in the Labour Party, because I remember meeting some of them myself, who spoke about the continuation of the wartime coalition in response to Churchill's appeal. These things didn't happen inexorably, they happened because a form of socialist, democratic and activist leadership was given at a critical moment.

Now the question is, can we mobilize in that way again? The answer is, we must. Because if we can't, then we are going to be locked into a permanent minority position while enormous damage is done to our society—we might even witness the destruction of our world community. So we have to work for the recreation of that sort of wide alliance attached to relevant policies which must be much more radical in socialist terms, and have a much stronger democratic dimension, than they had in 1945.

Well, I'm happy to hear that you don't believe this is inevitable—I don't either. Nevertheless, this brings us to the next question I want to put to you. This is to what extent the weaknesses and failures of the labour movement have aided this erosion of support, this gradual decline of support, and indeed dictated the failure, even after a year of the present government, of the movement— and, I would say, of the people as a whole—to recover the confidence that it should have in Labour. Now to what extent would you make the record of the various Labour governments between 1964 and 1979 responsible for this?

You know that I served in every Labour government from 1964 to 1979, and take my full share of responsibility for that. But it would be very foolish to deny that a heavy responsibility lies with the upper direction of the Labour Party over this whole period. That's why I mentioned the concept of surrender. Ideologically and tactically, there have been three waves of revisionism in the Labour Party over the last thirty years.

The first was the Gaitskellite wave, where it was argued, in broad agreement with Macmillan, that you could rely upon full employment and so sustain the welfare state without socialism. Every worker could have a mini in the garage, a television set in the living room and a package holiday in Majorca. Political trade unionism was no longer needed, and socialism was old hat. This revisionism was presented as Labour's response to Macmillan's 1959 victory. That was the first wave of revisionism: it took the form of a deliberate theological attack upon Clause 4 and was defeated, partly because the trade unions would have had to hold special conferences to change their own constitutions, many of which themselves included a version of Clause Four, and this would have been a bit of a nuisance.

The second wave came during the 1960s when Harold Wilson decided that the trade unions were an embarrassment to the Labour government, which was hoping to rise above its past as a product of trade unionism and present itself to the country as the natural party of government, strong enough to govern the country even when opposed by the trade unions.

The third wave of revisionism, which is now being vigorously resisted, is one based upon a coalition at the very top of the parliamentary and trade union leadership and designed to control the rank and file of the movement as reflected at Conference. This third wave is the most comprehensive of all because it is designed to consolidate, within the structures of the labour movement, an acceptance of the ideas of incorporation that were really defeated in May 1979. If that revisionism is accepted then we are finished. But it cannot, and will not, be accepted. That is why the argument is now focused primarily on internal democracy in the Labour Party. If we lost that battle, then the whole history of the labour movement would have culminated in a party with a Cape Canaveral–style rocket-launching function, its sole job being to fire the parliamentary leadership into orbit whenever there is a general election. Having discharged its function, the Labour Party, like the first stage of the rocket, would fall harmlessly into the Atlantic— that is not an acceptable role for the party and the movement.

One might have other criticisms of Wilson than the one you make. Wilson was I think very nearly the worst thing that has happened to the Labour Party, including Ramsay MacDonald, because he didn't even have the decency to leave it. I do think that there was more wrong with the Labour government in the 1960s than you suggest. One thing was that it didn't do anything, it didn't propose to do anything. In the 1964 election manifesto, there was a great deal about the white heat of technology which a lot of people believed—you yourself were not immune to this belief—and, of course, in some sense it was perfectly real, but there wasn't anything else. And, in fact, all the sorts of thing you might have expected a Labour government to do, such as updating the reforms of 1945–51, were not done.

That is a fair criticism. I don't think it was due to Wilson alone, or Gaitskell alone, or any single group of leaders. It was a collective development of revisionist thought that had become accepted in the Labour Party: the belief that full employment was permanent and that an expanding welfare state could always be financed by continuing full employment; that the finetuning of the mixed economy by a Labour government would always generate enough wealth and this could be redistributed in a rather more humane way, so that Labour governments working on that basis could progressively remove the inequalities and injustices of capitalism. There is no doubt that was the philosophy. If you read Harold Wilson's Conference speech on the white heat of technology it wasn't quite as naive as it's been made out. His argument about the white heat of the technological revolution was an expression of his belief that socialism had been made more relevant by science. He was also arguing that scientific change would have a serious effect upon people's lives, which would then have to be protected. He was saying that the white heat of technology was something that burned people and that therefore Britain would have to restructure and reorganize its industry and society in order to protect people from it.

But all that said, it is also true that in 1966, when Labour won a majority of one hundred in the Commons, consolidating its narrow election victory of October 1964, there was a complete reversal of engines and a return to absolutely traditional Treasury policies, followed later by an attack upon the power of the trade union movement which could not otherwise be contained within that sort of a policy for administering capitalism. That policy, plus Labour government support for America's war in Vietnam and various other decisions, did produce a collapse of support for the Party. Individual membership was virtually halved in those years, from 800,000 to 400,000.

Well, that brings me to another aspect of it which does involve you, since you are part of the Labour left. Both the Labour left and also perhaps the non-Labour left had their responsibilities, the Labour left particularly. What, in those years of Labour government, should the Labour left have done that they didn't do, what did they do that they shouldn't have done?

That is a very good question, because it touches on the crucial power that a Labour government has when in office: namely the power to call upon the loyalty of the Party to support it on the grounds that any succeeding Tory government would be much worse than the Labour government, whatever the latter did. This appeal to loyalty, which is perfectly understandable, can however be carried to the point where the role of Labour MPs and of the Party is reduced to the recording of a succession of votes of confidence.

What was beginning to happen during the period of the last Labour government was that the left was increasingly seeing the importance of developing socialism within the Labour Party as a party, in parallel with support for the Labour government as a government. I can cite as evidence, confirming the wisdom of that strategy, that the National Executive, which had been widely ignored for years as a rather powerless fan club of the parliamentary leadership, came to be seen by the Tory press and by the establishment, from 1975 onwards, as a serious centre of socialist thought and criticism, loyal to the government but critical of some of its policies. By contrast, if you look back at the minutes of the Labour Cabinet for 1931, you'll find that when Ramsay MacDonald consulted the National Executive about the crisis the NEC said it had little advice to offer, and would be content to leave everything to the Cabinet to decide—whereas at that time the TUC General Council was bitterly critical of what MacDonald was proposing.

Now if you compare that NEC response with the years of 1975–79, it is quite clear that the NEC and the Party formed a real centre of alternative policy that was loyal to the government but was critical, was creative, and was more forward-looking and socialist. The more I look back on that recent period the more I think that the role of the socialist critic of a Labour government must be to work within the Party, within the constituencies, within the trade unions, at Conference and in the National Executive and its study groups. That is the way to develop countervailing power in relation to a Labour government that will inevitably be under establishment pressure and will go wrong and will do the wrong thing from time to time. That is where the power of the left should be exercised, within the Labour Party rather than in futile gestures of pretending you are going to bring the government down, when of course, everybody knows you are not. For the left to bring down a Labour government would be the one crime that no one—quite properly—would ever forgive. That, it seems to me, is the answer to those who ask where the left should work, has worked, is working and where it is likely to be successful: in the Party.

I think you have made the answer to this question a little too easy, partly because it seems to me that your own left, or the sort of left that you represent is, if I may say so, a better Labour left than there has been for a very long time. And partly because it isn't really a question of the personal behaviour of individual ministers. What I was trying to get at is your reaction to the proposition that the Labour left in the sixties, and quite a long time before, really had no alternative policy?

That is a different argument. I am not sure that what you say is entirely true. In terms of nuclear weapons policy, public ownership and so on, the old left, if you like, of the 1960s was still existing and working during the 1970s. But the answer to your question about alternative policies arises from my earlier answer. It is because the left worked within the Party that it was able to develop the alternative policy. And the alternative strategy, which was accepted overwhelmingly at the recent Labour Party Conference at Wembley, was one that came out of the Labour Party, one to which the parliamentary leadership contributed very little and didn't really much believe in anyway. Moreover there is no doubt that in March 1974 a majority of the then Cabinet didn't really accept the manifesto on which they were elected. They had to accept that it was the manifesto because it had been developed within the Party and agreed with it, but I don't know that they really accepted it. However, the pressure to implement it was kept up by the Party. And it was a pressure for a consistent, logical, effective and relevant alternative policy. That was more useful than having a little parliamentary group always threatening to vote against a three-line whip but not able to reflect accurately the views of the Party in the country. So the left MPs did have a real alternative to advocate.

Of course one would accept that it's the right thing for the Labour left to operate within the Labour Party and, indeed, it's through the Labour Party and primarily through Labour governments that any social change that is likely to happen in this country is in the first instance going to be achieved. But that isn't quite the same thing as saying that the left within the Labour Party has an alternative policy and alternative solution. I think recently it has come closer than previously to having such a policy for a Labour government. Now, if I might make this a little bit more concrete, where do you situate yourself and the sort of people who think like you, compared to the older Labour left traditions, for example, the Bevan type of Labour left, the Keep Left Labour left, the Michael Foot type of Labour left? How do you see yourself as differing from them, or not differing from them?

Well, I think one difference between the two is that they were in a minority and we are in a majority. The questions of policy have been argued out in great detail since the 1972 Conference. I don't say that Conference policy is perfect because it clearly isn't, but it offers a reasonably consistent and different view about how the country's industry and economy should be run, how its social services should be developed, about the Party's internal democracy and about the role of Parliament. That view now has a majority position. So I suppose the biggest difference between the position which I find myself now, as compared to 1951 when Aneurin resigned, was that he was then in a minority and minorities—especially left minorities—can face great difficulty with the Party. At that time there was a clear majority in the TUC for traditional policies, and in the National Executive for right-wing or revisionist policies, and the Bevanite left never succeeded in getting a majority.

Now, of course, partly because the left couldn't get a majority, a lot of people who should now be in the Labour Party disappeared into community groups, into ultra-left movements and so on. Now that the Labour Party has got a majority around alternative—and socialist—policies, you are going to find that many of these people who left us in the sixties will be rejoining us. And that is going to consolidate the majority. So that that's the main difference. What the left were arguing at that time, looking back on it, seems to me very sensible.

I want to get back to this question of how to turn Labour back into a mass movement and a mass party. But, in the meantime, I would like to look at the question of this policy of yours. You say in Arguments for Socialism[2] and elsewhere that there are three or possibly four alternatives being put forward at the moment. There is monetarism, the Thatcher policy, there is something you call corporatism, there is democratic socialism, and there is what you regard as a non-starter, namely social democracy. Now while I think it is easy enough to see what monetarism means, because we hear it being expounded very clearly, I am not quite so certain what you understand by corporatism and I'm not very certain either that I understand what you mean by democratic socialism. The two things don't seem to me to be, as it were, of the same kind, fractions with the same denominator.

When I wrote that social democracy was a non-starter, what I meant was that the revisionism that was preached by Gaitskell and Crosland was killed, not by the left, but by the IMF, which simply said to the 1976 Labour Cabinet, 'We are not allowing you to do that any more. Whatever you choose to do, we are not having this high level of public expenditure because we regard it as undesirable'. Tony Crosland died six months after his social-democratic option had been killed for him by the IMF, and the IMF polished off revisionism fairly effectively. In 1976, I had hoped, when the IMF forced the choice between a socialist solution and a social-democratic defeat, that a Cabinet majority might be created for the more radical response. But that was not what happened. Monetarism, as you quite rightly say, is now being tried.

[2] Tony Benn *Arguments for Socialism* London 1979. Now available in Penguin paperback.

What I mean by corporatism is this: the centralization around the consensus politics that came from Harold Macmillan, Winston Churchill and Clement Attlee, who, during the wartime coalition, used William Beveridge, the Liberal economist, to set down the framework for post-war policy in employment and national insurance. That policy did succeed in its time, in part because of the destruction of our wartime enemies, because of a lot of conditions that won't recur, thus making full employment and the welfare state available. Even the nationalization of the basic industries was tolerated by the right in part because those industries had all failed—they weren't profitable any more, and if the state did reconstruct such basic industries, this would constitute a subsidy for private industry. So the post-war consensus had a certain solidity about it. But more recently we have seen the slump and the collapse of that consensus as an option. This collapse made those who believed in consensus huddle together more closely and become much more authoritarian. For example, both George Brown's and Edward Heath's pay policies began to develop some extremely authoritarian characteristics. So what I call the corporatist tendency, or however you want to describe it, is what happens when the consensus loses its grass-roots support and the people at the top have to huddle together to force their policies upon society in a more authoritarian way. It occurs when the people at the top decide what has to be done and the trade unions' function is to deliver their membership in pursuit of any agreement reached by their leadership. That was what Heath tried—unsuccessfully—to get the trade unions to do in 1973.

The particular characteristic of the British corporate state is that in this country medieval feudalism has lasted so long that it has fused with modern corporatism and created a most astonishing centralized bloc of political, financial and industrial power which has now virtually succeeded in defeating Parliament as an effective countervailing force, defeating Labour's rank and file, and commanding the general support of the civil service and the mass media. That is an authoritarian system. Mrs Thatcher very skilfully saw that she could do a re-run of the earlier attack on the feudal structure in the guise of recreating freedom for the entrepreneur. And she did it. She put on the *laissez-faire* armour of the early Adam Smith and cut through and won support. Corporatism now has no constituency except in the Golden Triangle of the City of London, Fleet Street and Whitehall. That's what I mean by corporatism.

Now you ask what democratic socialism is. It is an attempt first to find answers to the current problems of the crisis by defending working people against the policies of the government. It tries, through struggle, to generate a grass-roots leadership and a perception capable of carrying forward a policy that will reconstruct, and in parallel transform, the power relationships in industry and in society, not just as between capital and labour but as between government and governed. It is both a democratic and a socialist campaign that we are engaged in launching. And in the process it offers the prospects of recreating that winning coalition of 1945 that we spoke about. The Labour Party must align itself with the women's movement, the black movement, the environmental movement, the peace movement, the rural radical movement, the religious movements that object to monetarism and militarism, and bring back into the mainstream of the Labour Party those socialists who have been isolated in sectarian loneliness. That is the way I would present it.

If you ask what the specific policies are, well that's something we can argue about. But this is the broad conception. Capitalism is now log-jammed by an unresolved constitutional crisis between capital, government and labour. It is not open to us to make government run everything, because that would be authoritarian. Nor can we allow capital to ride rough-shod over us using monetarist policies. Labour now has to bring about the expansion of the public services and of our industry, by a socialist initiative that is possible only if there is a fully democratic Labour Party that will reflect Labour policies in the House of Commons. We need the recreation of the Labour Representation Committee, with a socialist dimension, at this period in our history. I think that's the way I would describe it.

I don't quite follow that, you see. I mean you are comparing different forms of breaking the log-jam, that is getting the British economy, and if you like, British society, moving again. Monetarism does so in Adam Smith's way or pretends to do so, by saying, let's go back to the market. Corporatism does so by control from above—bureaucratic control, I add—plus presumably some kind of economic policy which in the past has been a kind of Keynesianism.

Plus wage control—that is a part of a corporatist strategy.

Plus wage control, if you like. But how does democratic socialism come in? What is that self-discipline for democratic control of which you talk from time to time? I mean concretely. It's not that one isn't in favour of these things, but I would like to see exactly how it solves these specific problems that monetarism and corporatism purport to solve?

Well, every society requires discipline in order to operate. The discipline of the market is very clear: if it isn't profitable, it stops. The discipline of the corporate state is by legislation to determine what people are allowed and not allowed to do, including what wage claims they can put in and secure. The concept of democratic socialism is that by diffusion of power there will be a change in the relationships between capital and labour under the self-discipline of democratic control. Now that must involve, inevitably, a bigger role for the state, but not only by the state, nor by the state operating solely or principally at the national level.

For example, take the 1974 manifesto concept of the planning agreement, which was seriously weakened in cabinet between the February election and the publication of the white paper. Planning agreements were to make the power of the major corporations subject to the assent of the people who worked within them, without putting workers on the board. The concept of the tripartite planning agreement was that major companies would have to clear their corporate strategies with those they employed and they would not get a release of public money, via investment grants or regional employment premium or anything else, unless their plans had been agreed at the working level. That was a diffusion, not a centralization of power.

Why especially the people within them?

Because in the first instance capital has to be made accountable to the people it employs. That is not the only discipline there will be by any means, because the government will also be seeking to integrate—and this is a very early stage of a socialist transformation—the strategy of the major companies with the industrial policy of the government in the national interest. Take another example, which may offer a better answer to your question. The participation agreements that I compelled the oil companies to sign, were agreements under which the oil companies could only get their oil back from the government if they agreed to have their company strategy approved by the government. Now that was an accountability to the centre. But it was also my intention, and I began the process, to make those oil companies also accountable to the people they employed. That is a decentralization of power. If you ask for concrete examples of what we shall do when we come to power, depending when that is, remember we shall have inherited such a broken economy that what will then need to be done will be to take direct measures to recover and recoup the cuts in the public services; to invest directly in industry; to control imports into this country via a planned trade mechanism; and to retrieve from Brussels the power to determine our own industrial and economic policy; we shall also have to restore the power of parliament, especially by passing a Freedom of Information Act so that MPs and the public will be able to know what is happening.

I don't think it's difficult to think of concrete answers to concrete questions. What is difficult is to invest that policy with something that looks philosphically credible in answering an academic's question. I think I know what we would have to do. But what it would look like and how it would actually develop or what label you would feel, as an historian, you should attach to it, I'm not sure. But it would be democratic, not corporatist.

And it would not be monetarist. It would involve public initiatives, and it would involve a transfer of power from capital to labour and from government to parliament and also to localities and the regions. Now that you would have to define it when you saw it. What I have described is I believe a democratic socialist programme.

But that is exactly what my question is about, namely, what is concretely behind these phrases. These are not my labels, they are yours. What I want to know is their concrete meaning in terms of what you think ought to be done if Labour gets back. You know, I think it's marvellous, democracy, the more democracy the better—particularly, as you quite rightly said earlier on, now that we have got growing centralization, growing bureaucracy—and defence of this is necessary. Moreover I think this will be a very important way of regaining the political initiative and mass support. But at the same time, you see, democratic socialism as you put it is neither a policy nor a structure; it's a political style, democracy combined with an aspiration, socialism and social change. But what's in between?

I do not believe that democracy is just a matter of style. The most bitter battles in history have been about who should exercise power. And therefore I regard democracy as a very basic question. I am interested, for example, that the parliamentary leadership, or the right of the Labour Party, have never been much bothered if policy resolutions they dislike have been passed at Conference. They knew they could be neglected. But now that we are debating the structure of power in the Labour Party they recognize the importance of what is happening. Real political battles are all about democracy because democracy, plus an analysis and a proper sense of morality, are the main ingredients of socialism. Unless you believe that history offers you no democratic option—as in countries where there was no possibility of peaceful change, and there had to be a coup d'état in the name of socialism—the battles must be for democracy. What emerges after a revolution is not what I call socialism in this context. It would be a form of socialist corporatism, and socialist corporatism based on total public ownership is no more acceptable to me in a post-revolutionary situation than is the very mild sanitized Stalinism, in defence of the mixed economy, of the kind that we have had in British corporatism.

So I don't accept that democracy is just a matter of style, it's a matter of who is accountable to whom. And I think that if you present it this way, people understand precisely what you mean. They do not want to be just a platform for launching somebody else operating in their name into a position of power. They want to be sure when he or she is there that they are accountable for what they do. And this is a very important dimension of what we are saying.

You are totally right. Nevertheless, the question of power has very often, in the history of socialism, been made the excuse for saying we don't actually have to bother about what we are really going to do. Everybody said, from Marx on, the really important thing is how we are going to get there: what we are going to do after that is a hypothetical question which no doubt will be dealt with in concrete terms. The result is that when people get power, in one way or another, and I perfectly agree with you that in Britain it would have to be democratic, the question of what to do had to be started more or less from scratch. This is why I'm pushing you. It's clear, it seems to me, that what you are aiming at is, initially at any rate, a kind of mixed economy. You talk about renegotiation of terms between government and capital and labour. So in a sense it will go on initially being a mixed economy. How exactly is this going to be organized in such a way as to make a subsequent social transformation easier or more likely? What is the strategy of a social transformation—I don't say a transformation that would lead us to some hypothetical replay of the October Revolution because we would probably both agree that this is not really on. I'm not just trying to logic-chop.

I know you are not—and I am finding your questions very difficult. I would say this. Democracy is more than just a means of putting somebody into a position. If democracy was only how you got a government into power then I would agree with you, it would lose its significance.

And its accountability.

Yes—for remember, the corruption of power is a very real thing, in all structures. And democracy must be about what happens after you have won a majority, and not just an agency for getting a majority. There is one other point to make about being a Labour minister, where you are really a sort of worker on the board. Socialist ministers have got to strike the right balance between running society and changing it. If, when you get there, you simply run the system as it is, then you might just as well leave it to someone else who believes in the status quo to run it. If, on the other hand, you are always only talking about changing society, you may not meet the problems of workers as they face them and you lose your popular support. If people come to me with some urgent problem at a time when their employers are trying to close their works, and all I do is to read them a lecture on the need for socialist transformation, they would say 'this minister is no use to us, he's trying to use our crisis to advance his philosophy'. So you have got to run it *and* change it. And that is what the labour movement has got to make Labour ministers accountable for doing.

Now, a mixed economy? Yes, but a different sort of mix. Big companies—that means that 2 per cent by number, but about 75 per cent by output—must be either publicly controlled or publicly owned. When Aneurin Bevan redefined Clause 4 in terms of 'the commanding heights of the economy', he was redefining the mixed economy in terms of size. I think that's very important. Every little newsagent seems to have been persuaded that a left Labour government is going to nationalize them. We are not. The press have, for example, succeeded in deceiving the small shopkeeper into believing that he is under threat from a Labour government, and for the same reason as the big monopolies. The press has also persuaded every little family struggling to pay its mortgage that they and the big landowners are much of a muchness, both property-owners in a society challenged by rabid revolutionaries.

It is very important to define the mixed economy. The Labour Party believes that the hundred major companies have got to have statutory planning agreements in the first instance to release the power of labour within those companies, to make their management accountable, and to secure accountability to the national economic strategy. Public ownership has also got to be extended, not just to pick up the collapses of capitalism, long accepted as an ambulance function, but also as a way of getting public money into key areas of economic growth and development. Now I don't say that this is a comprehensive strategy for transformation, but at least it's got the twin goals of running the economy and changing it. The two roles have got to be kept in balance. Otherwise you are going to find you become either mere administrators of a declining capitalism, or just dreamers who are brushed aside because what you say is irrelevant to the daily needs of the man who is about to lose his job or the woman who is no longer able to get her child educated or can't get the facilities required for her family.

I think you are quite right to stress the importance of gaining and maintaining support, rather than simply announcing what you or I and a number of other people in this room may regard as desirable, and this brings me to the last question. It's exactly this mass support and this mass dynamism that is lacking in the Labour Party at the moment. How can we all get it back again?

Well I mentioned one of the ways. We must be very clear that we are not interested in a narrow, sectarian, purist Party all taking one view. You may have noticed that now the left is beginning to get a majority on the National Executive, we are deliberately limiting the grounds for expulsion. I think that what the left is now saying is that we want a very broad church, The condition for membership of the broad church, however, is that groups within the Party don't put up candidates against Labour candidates.

When you say broad church, do you mean a broad church of different tendencies within the Labour Party?

Yes. I think we must be a broad church. We have got a lot of different groups in the Labour Party. For example on the right we have the 'exitists' who have gone, we've got the 'departurists' who are packing to go, we've got the 'ultimatists' who will go if certain things happen, we have got the 'confrontationists' who have stayed to fight it out. But all these are in a minority. The solid core of the Party is socialist. I think it's important to remain broad because all the groups have got something to contribute to our work. But more than that, I want to broaden the Party out much further. I want to extend affiliations. Why if we are trying to get the NUT to affiliate, shouldn't you try to get the Indian Workers' Association to affiliate? Why if you are trying to get NALGO to affiliate, shouldn't you seek to persuade the women's movement to affiliate? I would like to see affiliations now open on a very broad basis, including the peace movement, the ecological movement and so on. In that way we will broaden the Party.

We must however be careful to see that the Labour Party, at this stage in its development, doesn't so excite the middle-class radicals that they come in and swamp our basic working-class support. That is why it is so important to build up factory branches, to expand basic political education. The Labour Party Commission of Inquiry has done a very good job on organization, finance and political education. We must also win the battle of Party democracy. If the trade union movement is to be induced to take a new and deeper interest in socialism— which is a precondition for mass support and social change— trade union members must be able to be sure that the policies that go through Party Conference will actually be in the manifesto and will be implemented by accountable parliamentary leaders.

If we get all those elements right—a broad Party; an effective organization to allow the trade unions to play a more active part in the Party; and a capacity to translate policy into action by using a parliamentary leadership that remains accountable—then I think we have a chance of success. I can't put it higher than that. But at least the Party is now beginning to understand where it went wrong and what it must do to put matters right. If we succeed we shall be able to answer the question that we get when we go canvassing. You knock at the door and they say, 'well we agree with you about all this, but how do we know that you are going to do it next time?' Until we can answer that question confidently we won't get the third dimension of mass support from people, especially from the working class, who are neither active trade unionists nor active Labour Party people but who really want to know whether it's going to be exactly the same next time as it was last time. We must be able to answer that question credibly to get the electoral majority necessary to breath life into the policies that we have been talking about.

But are you not—with all respect and with all my support for what you have said—looking at this in a little too narrow an organizational sense? Isn't the problem also how to get back the 33 per cent or so of the workers who voted for Thatcher? How to get the support from those people who are no longer members of the old blue-collar industrial working class on which the Labour Party based itself? How can we all turn the Labour Party into a party that speaks for the nation in the way that, once upon a time in, I think, 1940, the Tory people asked Arthur Greenwood to 'Speak for Britain'. Now you see the Labour Party is a class party of the workers. It's a party of the broad alliance of working people. But if the Labour Party is to become the party of the people once again it must once again be able to speak with credibility about the things that worry people, to speak for Britain. Can this be done simply by the democratization of the internal constitution of the Labour Party, however desirable that is, and by the correct toleration of the variety of things within it?

I don't think democracy or the institutions of democracy, of themselves, guarantee a particular outcome. If they did, one would be supporting whatever government had been elected. But I do think that one of the characteristics of the British establishment over the last few years has been its total defeatism about the future of Britain. The Vichy spirit has inhabited Whitehall over many many years since Arthur Greenwood was appealed to to speak for Britain. And the defeatism that characterizes the British ruling class has often struck me. I think they have got a slight whiff of self-confidence now from Mrs Thatcher, but they are frightened that she is going to overdo it, and that they will be back in trouble again.

But if you consider the fact that Britain has handed over a great deal of control of its industrial policy to the multinationals, a lot of control of our economic policy to the IMF, the control of many of our laws to the Common Market, and the effective control of our power to make peace and war to the United States, or NATO, you realise what an astonishing collapse of national self-confidence there has been amongst the establishment and what an erosion of democratic control has occurred under a succession of British governments, all of which were elected by the people of the United Kingdom. I don't believe in nationalism or a nationalist policy. Labour is a party with a strong international working-class tradition. But democratic self-government and liberation are as legitimate an aspiration for the British people as for the people of Zimbabwe or India or Guyana or anywhere else. Britain is now the last colony left in the British Empire. George Washington got out in 1776, Robert Mugabe got out in February 1980. Britain alone it seems is left with a colonial-type administration led by an establishment which is itself defeatist and is actually frightened of the potentiality and strength of the British labour movement working through parliamentary democracy. They have handed over the keys of power to others outside this country to govern us so that they can be protected from the British working class. An unconscious awareness, a sense that this has happened, is now embedded in the minds of an awful lot of British people. Unless and until they feel that a government is going to be returned to power that will put self-government and democracy into its programme and mean it, they may not even think that Labour would speak for Britain. That is a very important consideration. A strong democratic view of the future of Britain and the restoration of the powers of the British people to govern themselves, within an interdependent world society and with international responsibilities, is an integral part of the process of Labour's becoming a mass party. We must appeal to those who have voted Liberal or Conservative and to other working people who have deserted the Labour Party in the past because they felt it wasn't doing a proper job of representing them.

Well just let me say in conclusion that I think we probably agree on what needs to be done. I think we agree on the urgency of it. I think we agree that it has not yet been done nor have we entirely found the ways of doing it. And I hope, finally, we do agree that everybody on the left has a share in tackling this task and I hope we agree that all people on the left, whatever their views, had better concentrate their fire on their adversaries rather than on each other as they are in the habit of doing.

3

Steve Jefferys

Eric Hobsbawm uses three indices to support his argument that the forward march of labour ended between 1949 and 1953: trade union membership, the Labour vote and the quality of industrial struggle. He is factually wrong on trade union membership. While there has been a massive structural shift away from the traditional manual working-class occupations, as shown in Table 1, trade union consciousness (membership, as dem-

Table 1

Structural change in the labour force since the Second World War

	Percentage of wage earners employed	
	1948	1976
Mining, quarrying, metal manufacture, shipbuilding, mechanical engineering, textiles, railways	20.6	11.8
Electrical engineering, motor vehicles, tractors and cycles, aircraft manufacture	4.7	6.8
Business services, distribution	12.1	17.0
Education, medical and dental, local and national government services	12.0	21.3

onstrated in Tables 2 and 3, and strike activity, Table 4) has been more widespread in the 1970s than fifteen or thirty years ago. Women and black workers have been recruited to trade unionism at a faster rate than their white male counterparts,

Table 2

Trade union membership in the UK, 1967–78

	Year	Membership (000s)	Density (%)	Increase on 1967 membership (%)
Women	1967	2,286	27.2	—
	1975	3,464	36.6	51.5
	1978	3,789	38.2	65.7
Men	1967	7,908	53.0	—
	1975	8,729	60.7	10.4
	1978	9,322	64.9	17.9

and have strengthened rather than weakened 'class solidarity'. The comparison with the United States in Table 3, the only other major capitalist economy to escape both fascism and wartime occupation, highlights the fact that something happened in Britain in the decade after the mid-1960s, something that has been totally missed by Hobsbawm. Hobsbawm's use of electoral statistics is also flawed—though in a different way. He assumes that the Labour Party in 1951 was the *same* party that workers voted for in far fewer numbers in 1979. This, of course, is simply not so. In the 1940s the Labour Party was a predominantly working-class organization standing for *reform*; in the 1970s it is a largely middle-class organization standing for capitalist *rationalization*. Hobsbawm has already conceded that he 'may well have been wrong' in presenting his third index, sectionalism, as being stronger today than in 1951.

Thus all his three indices of 'advance' are awry. Why then is the debate important? Basically, because Hobsbawm's uneasy foray into post-1950 labour history raises some tricky questions for socialists in today's labour movement: is the Communist Party's thirty-year-old concept of an 'advance' down a 'British road' to socialism valid, and why is the movement in a mess today? What sort of a mess is it, and what can be done about it?

In 1951, the moment from which Hobsbawm dates his 'halt', the

[1] *The British Road to Socialism*, 1951, p. 14.

Table 3

Trade Union density in the US and the UK since the Second World War

	US		UK	
	Total trade unionists (millions)	per cent of labour force	Total trade unionists (millions)	per cent of labour force
1948			9.4	45.8
1950	14.3	22.0		
1955	16.8	24.4		
1956			9.8	44.5
1965	17.3	22.4		
1966			10.1	42.5
1976	19.4	20.1	12.4	54.9

Communist Party formalized its view of the British revolution as a 'road' down which an alliance of Labour Party militants and the Communist Party would gradually 'advance' into the socialist dawn: 'The enemies of Communism accuse the Communist Party of aiming to introduce Soviet Power in Britain and abolish Parliament. This is a slanderous misrepresentation of our policy. Experience has shown that in present conditions the advance to Socialism can be made just as well by a different road. . . . the British Communists declare that the people of Britain can transform capitalist democracy into a real People's Democracy, transforming Parliament, the product of Britain's historic struggle for democracy, into the democratic instrument of the will of the vast majority of her people'. Well, if this is your measuring stick, time has indeed stood still. 'Experience' has shown that the key struggles of the 1960s and the 1970s have almost all taken place outside parliament and the parliamentary process: the campaigns for nuclear disarmament and against the war in Vietnam, the fight against the Industrial Relations Act, the struggles at Upper Clyde Shipbuilders and Grunwick, the Anti-Nazi League, to name just a few. And today's Thatcherite parliament is, perhaps, the most representative of the *ruling* class since 1945.

The Communist Party's map, however, has two secondary roads feeding into the main trunk road to socialism: the Labour-CP alliance road, for which the winning of influential union leaders is central; and the road of 'union power'. It is Hobsbawm's denial of a forward march down these roads that has created such a stir within the CP. This is because the latter has repeatedly claimed advances on these two secondary roads and has read them in between the lines of countless TUC and Labour Party resolutions. In 1954, John Gollan was writing: 'Broadly speaking, the struggle of the militant forces in the Labour Party and the trade union movement, despite differences and confusion, is an effort to reverse the official reformist line which is leading to disaster.' And after describing the new 'left' trade union block vote at the 1953 Margate Labour Party Conference, he concluded: 'The alliance (with the majority of constituency parties) will grow and develop and is the key to the transformation of the situation in the Labour Party.'[2]

Twenty-five years later, Mick Costello, the CP's present industrial organizer, argues that the rate of progress down these two secondary roads is synonymous with the 'advance to socialism' itself: 'The British Road to Socialism . . . correctly sees advance in terms of building the movement that can, in the course of the revolutionary process, end capitalist exploitation.'[3] So, like Ken Gill by defining 'forward march' as 'building the movement'—without specifying any immediate *socialist* content to that growth—he can even find 'advances' under the 1974–79 Labour Government: 'This was also the period of the repeal of the Industrial Relations Act and the enactment of legislation which prompted equality for women and encroached upon the employers' power to sack at will. These are advances of a political character fully in line with the strategy of the *British Road to Socialism*.' A repeal made inevitable by mass strike action, pathetic equal pay and

---

[2] *The British Political System*, p. 173.
[3] *Marxism Today*, June 1979.

opportunities legislation, 'encroachment' on the right to hire and fire by a Labour government presiding over a rise in unemployment of one million . . . these are 'advances to socialism'! It is easy to see why Hobsbawm shouted 'Enough'. Only those blinded by the need to justify their past and present activity can fail to appreciate the savagery with which the last Labour Government attacked living conditions, employment, the social services, and the independence of Britain's rank-and-file trade union system.

One of those recently 'sacked at will' was Derek Robinson. While Longbridge convenor he was convinced that 'workers' participation' within British Leyland was one such 'advance . . . fully in line with the British Road': 'If we make Leyland successful it will be a political victory. It will prove that ordinary working people have got the intelligence and determination to run industry.'[4] What the incorporation of the senior stewards in participation schemes did, in fact, was to pave the way for the isolation of the stewards from the membership. Bullock and Donovanization (the execution of the 1968 Donovan Commission's proposals to weaken the power of sectional shop stewards by providing facilities and power to a factory-based layer of senior stewards to work within a framework of written agreements, productivity deals and procedures) were clearly not 'advances' of any description. Their *form* gave more personal prestige to some 8,000 full-time lay convenors and branch officials: to these people (and to the TUC in their cosy relationship with government) it appeared that the trade union movement was getting more recognition. But their *content* was an attack on organization, ideas and action that put workers' immediate interests first, and was independent of the corporate goals of the company or of the 'national interest'.

Rank-and-file trade unionism was being weakened by a partly successful *incorporationist* strategy at the very moment when some argued that 'the movement is stronger now than at any time in its history' (Gill). This confusion comes easily to those who see the struggle for socialism as a 'road' or a 'process'

[4] *Comment*, August 5, 1978.

rather than as a daily struggle for power, whose closest analogy is continuing trench warfare where there are defeats and victories, ground lost and taken, and prisoners captured, and in which progress can only be recorded when decisive defeats are inflicted on the enemy. The confusion is not a new one. It has been at the centre of the debate between revolutionaries and reformists in the labour movement in Britain for a hundred years. And it is also at the heart of the major issue raised by Hobsbawm: the nature of today's crisis.

Hobsbawm is clearly right to point to the fact of a crisis: the ease with which Robinson was victimized, the absence of generalized resistance to unemployment, the disintegration of the Broad Left in key unions (as shown by the crushing defeat of Bob Wright in the 1980 AUEW Presidential election), the erosion of the self-confidence of the shop stewards' organizations of the 1960s and early 1970s, the rate of decline of the CP's membership (which has far outstripped the growth of the Socialist Workers' Party and the rest of the revolutionary left). All these are signs of one aspect of the crisis: the significant shift to the right in trade union politics since 1974. But the crisis is a dual one. Thus, despite this shift to the right, the rank and file, workplace-based core of British trade unionism remains at the centre of the British capitalist crisis. It continues to present the British ruling class with its biggest obstacle to achieving the elusive 'economic miracle' it has pursued with increasing ferocity for the last fifteen years. Thus in 1980 rank-and-file steelworkers mounted militant flying pickets, Gardners' workers occupied against sackings, and Leyland's Longbridge workers finally won a vote for strike action. Let us look at how this dual crisis developed. In the twenty years after the Second World War the British ruling class found it more convenient (and profitable) to live with the workplace-based trade unionism that emerged from wartime conditions. Strikes were small and short. Shop stewards' organization grew within the limited horizon of the factory walls: they felt no need to build bridges between factories or to pay much attention to the official machine or to politics. As world capitalism moved in synchronized crisis, and

British capitalism grew noticeably sicker, state intervention in industrial relations became more frequent: wage controls, unemployment and anti-union laws were used by both the Wilson and the Heath governments of the 1960s and 1970s to try to encourage higher productivity and profits, and so to stimulate new investment. This political attack on a confident but fragmented working class shook the fragments into shape.

Between 1969 and 1974, four qualitative developments took place: (1) tactics such as occupations and flying pickets were used, which challenged management's 'right to manage' more directly than other traditional sanctions; (2) solidarity strikes re-appeared for the first time since 1926; (3) there were around thirty national or local token political strikes; (4) trade union consciousness was generalized to a significant extent among white-collar and black and women workers. For a time the Chinese wall between economic and political industrial action was placed under siege. Fragmentation and sectionalism still coexisted alongside solidarity strikes by miners in support of the nurses, but among an active minority of workers a class consciousness emerged with a political radicalism unknown since the 1920s. Table 4 compares the upsurge of class combativity in 1969–74 with Hobsbawm's 'advanced' period, 1949–53 and with the record of 1977–79. The Heath Government was

Table 4

Strikes: 1949–53, 1969–74 and 1977–79

	Annual Average		
	1949–53	1969–74	1977–79
Number of stoppages	1,589	2,924	2,418
Workers involved per strike	365	540	929
Days lost per striker	3.1	8.2	7.3
Aggregate number of days lost (000s)	1,773	12,872	16,340

ultimately defeated, not by the Labour opposition, but by the miners, by the refusal of the rest of the trade union movement to break ranks, and by the rejection by a narrow majority of voters of the argument that the unions had too much power.

The present crisis is the direct consequence of the movement's inability in 1974–79 to transform the struggle from one against a *Tory* definition of the 'national interest' into a fight against a Labour version. Its unity turned out to be unity against Heath. Despite the objective need to maintain the class offensive in the face of a Labour government, the movement collapsed back into its fragments. Most of those who had been politically radicalized between 1969 and 1974 were either in the CP or the Labour left or—a still larger number—were influenced by them. And their argument was that *the* vehicles for building upon the ruling-class defeat that had just taken place were the 'left' union leaders, Jones, Scanlon and Daly, or the 'left' Labour election programme of 1974. Those who argued for building *rank-and-file* organizations within and between different groups of workers to try and preserve some wider form of class solidarity and the capacity to act independently of the rightward moving trade union bureaucracy, were easily dismissed as 'ultra-left'.

When, therefore, in the recession of 1975–76 inflation doubled to over 20 per cent and unemployment climbed from 600,000 to a new 1.4 million plateau, the movement that had resisted Heath's Phase 3 in 1974 now embraced Wilson's Social Contract. Those in a position to do so had made no political organizational preparations to withstand anti-working-class Labourism. And the industries that had led the 1969–74 upsurge—the car industry, shipbuilding, engineering, the docks—were hit hardest, while the Broad Left union leaders gave unqualified support to the Social Contract.

Militancy on its own had worked in the 1950s and 1960s; militancy in a class-wide fight against the Tories had worked in the early 1970s. But within the workplace walls, in the face of wage cuts and sackings presented as inevitable by the government in alliance with the AUEW, TGWU and NUM, militancy now appeared ineffective. Fragmented and isolated, in the political context of the Social Contract, many more senior stewards jumped at an apparent alternative to impotence: full-time status with consultation or participation in company policy-making. The pace of Donovonization accelerated. Resentments against Labour's anti-working-class policies were thus denied expression through both the trade union bureaucracy and large sections of the fragmented shop stewards' organizations. For some sections of workers the promise of tax cuts under the Tories appeared to meet their rising bills.

While the Social Contract weakened trade unionism, it gave the ruling class a valuable breathing space. An open employers' offensive then resumed when it became obvious that despite the good offices of the TUC, the Labour government would not be able to deliver the third and fourth phases of the Social Contract. The resistance of Grunwicks, Sandersons and Garners to lengthy union recognition strikes in 1977 and 1978 was the tip of the iceberg. The right-wing National Association for Freedom actually mobilized thousands of small businessmen behind active strike-breaking. From 1977 on, employers increasingly resorted to the courts against unions and pickets. In 1978 the CBI abandoned 'consensus' incomes policy; in 1979 the Engineering Employers' Federation felt confident enough to issue guidelines on lock-out action against any form of internal dispute. And in 1980, without any degree of resistance, the Tories put the Employment Act on the statute book and gave the police and the employers the legal incentive to dismantle effective picketing and solidarity action.

Of course, the continuing strength of shop-floor trade unionism meant that this ruling-class offensive met with a new upturn of resistance. But unlike the early 1970s, this time the response never went beyond militant sectionalism. The Broad Left in the AUEW—the brightest feather in the cap of CP industrial strategy—was defeated and demoralized. The state of the Liaison Committee for the Defence of Trade Unions was similarly pathetic by comparison with 1969–71: neither organization coped with the retreat of the left trade union bureaucracy. Thus from the firemen to Fords and the steelworkers, each section fought on its own. And after the steel strike, as the recession bit even harder than in 1975-76 and unemployment moved toward 2½ million class combativity slumped to a new low.

The mess is thus essentially political. The strength of British trade unionism for over thirty years has been its base in the workshops, depots and offices, its tradition of local democracy and hence its unpredictability and independence. But these qualities are not sufficient in the face of a world capitalist crisis and a British capitalism dominated by multinational capital. The CP's Broad Left/labourist strategy is not sufficient either. For thirty years CP members were the most prominent members of the 'club' of rank-and-file militants. But from 1974 to 1979, the limits of rank-and-filism on its own, coupled with the CP's orientation towards the bureaucracy, carried the heavy price actually being noted by Hobsbawm: the collapse of the CP's industrial base as the guiding centre for militants without its replacement by any alternative left centre.

Our present problems—sackings, wage cuts, butchery of the welfare state—cannot be solved by do-it-yourself reformism in the workplace. Nor can they be solved by leaving politics to the Labour Party and the trade union bureaucracy, or by drawing up plans to make British capitalism viable. The last thirty years have proved, surely beyond doubt, the bankruptcy of labourism. What is needed is to harness the rank-and-file strength of the movement to clear, class-wide socialist objectives: to raise the banner of the fight against capitalism in the context of the struggle within it. This, of course, is not a simple mechanical task. Every struggle has a potential that can be generalized. There's no pat formula for guaranteeing that it's done. But what socialists can do is to adopt the right *strategic* approach.

If we are right that the most unpredictable and explosive area of the British labour movement is its rank and file, then that's where we should concentrate. Whether we're building support for the Right to Work Campaign, for a mass picket in defiance of the Employment Act, or for a demonstration against racism and fascism, what really counts is organization from below. And today, that means really working on the basics: the respect of picket lines, collections for others on strike, solidarity action, rebuilding the independence of shop stewards' committees, building united-front rank-and-file organizations to generalize the anti-Tory fight.

If Hobsbawm is still looking for the Andy Capp class consciousness of the white, male, Labour-voting craftsmen of the AEU and ETU when they were under CP control in the 1940s, then he will continue to miss what is happening. But if he turns to look to the black and white, male and female, manual and white-collar working class of today and examines *their* rebellion,[5] he will at least know what it is that socialists have to insert their organization and ideas into.

---

[5] Articles in *International Socialism Journal*, 5, 6, 7, by myself, Tony Cliff and Dave Beecham, debating the post-war labour movement and the present crisis, have all contributed to the analysis sketched above, and should be read by anyone wanting to learn more about the views of the Socialist Workers' Party.

Bob Wright

I welcome Eric Hobsbawm's analysis of the history and current state of the British labour movement, and also the debate to which it has given rise. Such discussions are made all the more timely by the resurgence of political controversy inside the Labour Party and the constitutional changes to which this has led. The significance of these changes may be underlined by a brief review of the political dimension of the relationship between the party and the trade unions, and between the leaderships of both and the movement as a whole.

'The ending of the system that creates unemployment and poverty in the midst of plenty' became the maximum demand in the early years of this century, as a patriotic, reformist, and in many senses bourgeois, craft unionism gave way before the politically challenging growth of the new unions. The trade unions took up the call for labour representation in parliament. The Labour Party as it then emerged was moulded from trade unions, socialist societies and local trades councils and Labour Representation Committees. It was not until 1918, after a bitter struggle against an essentially corporate leadership, that provision was made for individual membership. The opportunity to create a class party was amply available in this period of the labour movement's development—a period characterized by economic crisis and marked by the Russian Revolution and the upsurge of proletarian struggles in Europe. But the period that followed was the most telling one in Labour's history. Internal divisions resulted in the exclusion of Marxist elements and the Communist Party was launched. Lenin's earlier description of a 'parasitic labour aristocracy' was quite apparently true of a party which, although it retained a radical and class-conscious base, was largely an 'appellant' organization destined for corporate integration within the system, which it genuinely sought to manipulate to the benefit of the working class. Reformism prevailed, and although Labour's unique combination of trade-union and political organization was potentially of great value, the party entered the twenties with a clear division between the parliamentary-union leadership and the wider movement that was to remain until 1945.

Perhaps the most vivid example of this division was given by the imprisonment in 1921 of the socialist members of Poplar Borough Council for their refusal to impose rates on the blighted population of the district in order to meet a London County Council levy. Their crime was a refusal to cut relief to the poor and unemployed; but Herbert Morrison deplored their action and J.H. Thomas denounced them as 'wastrels'. The case of Poplar was not unique. The defeats of 1926 and 1931 were clear and predictable products of the 'bipartisan' policies that linked the Labour leadership to the Liberals and the Conservatives. The resulting toll on the organization, finances and membership of the trade unions led their leaders to adopt a protective stance and made them extremely wary of giving support to the rank-and-file movements that had emerged in the forms of militant shop stewards' committees and trades councils, and so, much of the struggle of the unemployed passed under Marxist or rank-and-file leadership. It is not widely accepted, but I believe it to be true that the depression and mass unemployment of the twenties and thirties caused a centralization of power in the trade unions and consolidated Labour's parliamentary bourgeoisie as we know it today—and led also to the practice of witch-hunting those who were prepared to challenge its authority. Equally, of course, it would be wrong to deny the great contribution of the labour movement to the struggle for socialist policies, its early support for the Russian Revolution and, later, its defence of the Spanish Republic against fascist counter-revolution—or, for that matter, its mobilization against fascism in Britain. All these struggles gave evidence of a political awareness in Labour activists which, I believe, is still alive today.

In any examination of Labour's role from 1945 onwards it is essential to appreciate the structure of the ruling class in Britain, in particular the extent to which the right wing of the labour movement has been absorbed into it. The resounding electoral victory of 1945 gave new impetus to the politics of democratic socialism, and the experience of the war against fascism drew the left together to carry forward a programme of major social reforms. The concept of public ownership seemed a powerful means of economic control; the need for a major reconstruction of society brought new demands for equality of opportunity and equal rights in education; and the maintenance of peaceful coexistence pointed to new alignments in international relations. But 1948-49 proved a turning-point: policies of this kind were rolled back and capitalist priorities were reasserted with the acquiescence of Labour's leadership. The onset of the Cold War and the outbreak of hostilities in Korea were the signals that halted the forward march of labour and marked the return of bipartisanship in foreign affairs. Reactionary propaganda took its toll among many workers, no doubt, as a right-wing order re-established itself.

The fifties saw a massive development of pro-peace forces and continuing struggles to reaffirm socialist policies in the labour movement. But although gains were made in terms of conference decisions, it became clear that the persistence of Cold War policies was distorting the policies of the left not only in international affairs but also at home. I would argue very strongly that the circumstances of the fifties caused a major shift of emphasis in the left's campaigns: we increasingly abandoned the struggle for socialist policies and control of the leadership in favour of a new conception of rank-and-file power, whereby a somewhat anarchic resistance would bring about political progress. The sixties and seventies therefore saw the creation of a political vacuum that was filled, when it was filled at all, by far-left groupings whose academic-student base led them often to ignore the working class and whose activities sometimes made them easy targets for ruling-class propaganda meant to discredit the left as a whole. Encouraged by the purely economist militancy described by Hobsbawm and by this political vacuum, the Tories and the right-wing Labour leaders launched their offensive against the trade unions, setting out first to discredit militant shop stewards and then to impose legal sanctions designed to tame activism generally. Resistance was mounted in the 1968-74 period and later in the public sector, but fundamentally the offensive was a success.

1972 saw the beginning of a concerted fightback against the betrayals of the trade-union and party leaderships, as the Labour left and Marxist minority embarked on a campaign to demand accountability and a new organizational structure through which to assert a positive role for the rank and file in the formation of Labour Party policy. This growing demand for democratic control, which has so far produced the constitutional changes agreed at the 1980 Conference and extraordinary conference of January 1981, is central to any effort to resume the forward march of labour.

Deliberate media distortion has meant that even now there are many trade unionists who seem not to appreciate fully the importance of party democracy to the trade-union movement. There was little point in going to party conferences and voting for resolutions calling for cuts in runaway defence budgets, for increased public expenditure and withdrawal from the EEC when we did not have the means to ensure that such policies would be included in the manifesto and then implemented by a Labour government. None of these policies could have been passed in the first place without massive support from the union delegation; it seems obvious that if the unions will the end they should also will the means. These means are constitutional changes providing for mandatory re-selection of MPs, election of the party leader by an electoral college, and control of the manifesto by Conference and the National Executive Committee. They are essential if we are to avoid a repetition of such disasters as the incomes policy imposed by the Callaghan government against the wishes of both the TUC and the Party Conference.

A Labour government is elected to serve the interests of

working people, not to demand useless sacrifices from them in order to prop up an economic and social system that has left British workers among the lowest paid in Western Europe with our industrial base gradually crumbling away. The next Labour government will inherit an economic crisis of terrifying proportions, and in order to confront it the entire labour movement must be united. But such unity can be achieved only if conference decisions are honoured by the government, if the leadership marches in step with the rank and file. This is the real significance of the campaign for democratic accountability in the Labour Party, and this is its political potential.

Bernard Dix

Eric Hobsbawm suggests that the labour movement has passed into crisis. This immediately poses the question: what *kind* of crisis? Put the issue to most trade-union leaders and they would point to post-war experience, in the years until the middle or late 1960s, and say: 'On the contrary, there is no crisis at all'. During that period they had won positions of power from which they demanded effective consultation through which they could influence the decisions of both Labour and Conservative governments. Over the same period, and partly because of these developments, the material living standards of the working class improved significantly. Can this be summarized as a 'crisis'? I would argue that if there is a crisis, then it is not of the kind implied in such responses. It has to do precisely with the apparent progress of the post-war period and what it entailed; a very pragmatic approach in the trade-union movement and dilution of the class content of the Labour Party. The problem is, whether the whole political direction the movement has taken represents an advance or a retreat.

It is being argued that certain trends in trade-union practice represent a significant change for the worse in political direction: above all, the trend—discussed by Hobsbawm—towards 'sectionalism'. Our union, NUPE, was very sharply attacked for this during the so-called Winter of Discontent of 1978–79. It would be absurd to assert that trade unions never pursue sectional interests regardless of the consequences for the class as a whole; basically, people join unions to protect their own conditions of work, and you can't simply submerge this fact in deeper political considerations. But I would deny that trade unions *increasingly* act in a sectionalist way. On the contrary, they have tended to seek broader bases of action, and this is particularly true in the public sector. In 1975, NUPE and thirteen other public service unions organized a Committee Against the Cuts, through which they have campaigned against cuts in public services *not* on the basis that they affect the job interests of our members—we look after those in our ordinary union activity—but because of the social and economic consequences of the cuts for the community as a whole. We have tried also to relate to the labour movement as a whole, to demonstrate to unions in the manufacturing and construction industries what cuts really mean for their members, not only as users of the services our members provide but as producers of the capital goods the services themselves require. Year after year, we have tried—with some success among our own members—to emphasize the underlying unity between workers in the public services and those in manufacturing industry; they rely on us for a whole range of community services, while we depend on a strong manufacturing base to generate the wealth to finance those services. The real failing of the 'Winter of Discontent'—which was a fight against the cuts as well as a fight for pay—was that we had not been able, at that time, to impact our message on the whole movement—much less on the Labour government.

Nevertheless, it is argued by anti-trade union forces that trade unions today are not like their predecessors, who prized and practised working-class solidarity. It is true that today a strike by a handful of workers can close a factory employing thousands; but this is only half the story. What is often condemned as 'sectionalism' is very often the spontaneous effect of technological changes that have given decisive power to small groups of workers; it's not that the workers have become bloody-minded, but that the productive process is changing and this has implications on the actions of many people and presents a challenge to the traditional tactical wisdom of the unions.

As NUPE grew in size and self-confidence, through the sixties and into the seventies, we had to meet this challenge directly; not because of technological change but because of the kind of union we are. Our problem was two-fold. First, there were areas of work in which strike action on our part could have very serious consequences for the working class and the community generally; health care is the most obvious case. Second, at the opposite pole, there were areas where our members could strike for ever without having the smallest effect on the employers—the public parks, for instance. We didn't want to cause unnecessary suffering, and as a consequence provoke antagonism, and we didn't want to dissipate our energies and morale by calling out workers who had little or no impact on the outcome of an action. So, we had to go beyond the old slogan of 'one out, all out' and to think of struggles utilizing a multiplicity of tactics.

During one strike, for example, we agreed that the ambulance crews would continue to answer emergency calls. But the employers responded by saying to the ambulance crews: 'If you don't do the full range of duties, we're going to send you home', which meant there would be no ambulance services at all. The fact that our members were prepared to maintain emergency services was used against them, and it was very difficult to convey this to the public because of the hostility of the press towards our union. During strikes by hospital ancillary workers our branches have set up committees who discussed with management and the medical staff what patients would be dealt with so that urgent and emergency cases were covered. Operating theatre lists supplied by the medical staff were reviewed, and all vasectomies, for example, were deferred for the duration of the strike. A very high degree of flexibility and cooperation was required to maintain critical areas of service, and it showed strength, not weakness, in our members, that they were able to demonstrate a kind of working-class discipline in the face of inexperience and extreme pressure.

Selective striking is another tactic our union has employed. In 1970, as part of a rolling programme of extending strike action, we called out the refuse-collectors in one of the London boroughs. A local organizer reported back to say that they had decided that only the drivers were coming out while the rest of the refuse gangs were reporting for work. There was nothing in the existing job agreement that said a crew could be laid off if no work was available; so there were half-a-dozen crews without drivers, helping the street sweepers, playing cards, getting their full pay every week and splitting it with the striking drivers. Similar actions by workers in other sectors have revealed the same growth of tactical creativity and sophistication among the membership. Indeed, it's partly recognition of this that has prompted right-wing demands for changes in the laws relating to industrial disputes.

However, this kind of concrete thinking and self-reliance would not have been possible twelve years ago. NUPE's organizational forms would not have permitted it. At that time we had a paternalistic structure that was a mirror-image of the public services themselves. For example, we had no shop stewards until 1969; before then no such office existed either in our rule book or in our agreements with the employers. In 1975, after several years of intense internal discussion, we held a special conference that turned the old structure upside down. We reorganized the union and built upwards from branch district committees consisting of stewards or branch secretaries, to area committees also consisting of stewards or branch secretaries, to divisional councils also consisting of stewards or branch secretaries. So, to move up through the union structure, a member must be actively involved at workplace level. This reorganisation was the union's response to its own massive growth—from 14,000 in the mid-thirties to 650,000 in the mid-seventies—and to the reorganization of the local government and NHS employers into much larger units. The initiative for this reorganization came from the Executive—'sponsored democracy', one academic called it at the time—and initially it provoked a fair amount of suspicion among the rank and file. But in practice it has increased the general level of consciousness and of confidence in the union, and has enabled it to absorb and make full use of the experience of specific struggles.

Our union was one of the first to use new tactics in industrial disputes, for reasons I have already indicated; but our experiences are there for the movement as a whole to reflect upon and learn from. The civil service unions have recently given very effective demonstrations of the use of highly selective industrial action and there is no reason why this could not be extended to other unions. Imagine, for example, a dock strike in which all exports would be stopped but imports of foodstuffs and other essentials would be unloaded as usual. These are merely illustrations but they indicate the kind of tactical development that can counter the charge of sectionalism in the labour movement. Such developments are within reach, given democratic internal discussion and accountability in the trade unions.

The industrial role of the trade unions is, however, only one aspect of organized working class activity. Another is their political role through the Labour Party. Hobsbawm devotes far less space to this topic, but he does point to 'the Wilson years' as a demoralizing political experience for many in the working class. This was very likely the case, but we should be clear about the reasons. Political expectancy in 1964 was nothing like it had been in 1945. The period of Tory rule between 1951 and 1964 wasn't remotely like—for example—the first two years of the present Thatcher government; it wasn't the kind of experience that generated extreme class passions. Wilson responded to this by going out of his way, before the 1964 election, to appeal to young middle-class voters. He fought the election on the basis that a Labour Government could cope with the age of the white-hot technological revolution. People didn't expect radical, fundamental change from the Wilson government, but they had been led to expect that Labour would be better able to direct the economy. That was the extent of Wilson's promise: 'We can *manage* the economy'. It became quickly apparent that his government *couldn't* manage the economy any better—or worse—than the previous Tory government, and was running into the same kind of difficulties and responding in the same general way as the Macmillan government had done. The marginal shifts at subsequent general elections reflected an underlying continuity in the policies and practices of governmental economic management; and when the radical break finally came it was not to the left at all but to the right, under the leadership of Thatcher.

This is the situation that the Social Democrats are hoping to exploit. They know—from the experiences of previous Labour and Tory Governments—that welfare capitalism cannot deliver the goods, and they sense that a fair portion of the electorate knows it too. At the same time, they know that people don't want the harsh social consequences of abrasive monetarism, so they are purporting to represent a third possibility which they are incapable of defining. This Social Democratic option may be unsubstantial but that does not mean that it will inevitably fail at the polls. Unless the leftward push in the Labour Party is sustained and translated into binding policy, all we can expect to see is competition in rhetoric between the Social Democrats and some wishy-washy right-wing Labour Party, with victory going to the more plausible performer. Who's got the slickest posters? Who's got the better telly image? Which Roy do you prefer: Hattersley or Jenkins? An election fought on these lines would be an absolute disaster.

The leftward push I am talking about is one of policy. It was because it proved impossible to get a Labour government to respond to attitudes existing in the movement that constitutional changes in the Party became necessary. There are a lot of people, at every level of the party, who seem to believe that the party outside parliament is merely an electoral machine, and that the proper function of party activists is to collect subscriptions and organize social clubs while a few party hacks preserve a skeleton organization that can be fleshed out and put into action at election time. The people who are looked upon as abnormalities, even among some party activists, are those who get up at meetings and propose resolutions or initiate discussions about policy. But working-class politics should not proceed simply by counting the number of votes cast for the party, or the number of seats won. If that were appropriate, all we would need to do—as some Labour politicians have done—is construct a platform on the basis of the lowest common denominator. The politics of the Labour Party must be based on the discussion and clear expression of a political philosophy, and the extent to which the Party moves forward will then depend not simply on votes and seats won but on the political basis upon which they are won. The recent constitutional changes are among the essential means to reverse the drift towards an American-style electioneering role for the party, in favour of the development of a principled, agreed and binding programme.

Social Democrats and the Labour right argue that the existence of the trade-union block vote contradicts the democratic claims made for these changes. But it is the privileged access of a few union leaders—a handful of the TUC General Council—to the Labour front bench and a Labour government which constitutes the real abuse of democracy. Informal discussions at this level frequently predetermine many major policy issues over the heads—and behind the backs—of union conferences, the Parliamentary Labour Party, and the Labour Party conference. And it was precisely because the party conference was unable to make any impact on the parliamentary party that the disproportionate influence of a few trade-union leaders on the parliamentary leadership was able to be maintained. That will no longer be the case; because the re-selection of Labour MPs will enable the party outside of parliament to impact on Labour's front bench—and this would be so even if the Wembley Conference decision were reversed and the leader elected by the MPs. One of the aspects of the constitutional changes to which the trade unions will have to adjust is that it will no longer be possible for the front bench to ignore the parliamentary party and yet accept what a handful of trade-union leaders are saying. If union leaders want to exert political influence, they will have to do so openly: through their own union machinery and through the party conference, debating the issues and accepting the vote on them. Gone are the days when a few heavy trade union leaders like Deakin and Lawther could effectively run the party conference without leaving their seats in the body of the hall because they had fixed it all beforehand. I suspect that a lot of the outrage expressed by Social Democrats and Labour right wingers over the block vote is in fact lament for the passing of the days when the leader of the Parliamentary Labour Party could depend on cosy relationships with a few right-wing union leaders—even to the extent of arranging for unions to overturn their votes on issues like German rearmament and unilateralism. The political significance of relationships such as these has been decisively reduced by the opening that has taken place.

All this has a bearing on the relation between the parliamentary and extra-parliamentary activities of the labour movement. Politics, to most people, is what goes on in the House of Commons. But experience has taught many workers—certainly NUPE members over the past five years—the relationship of politics to the jobs they do, and the importance of being able to influence the formation of political policies as well as pay levels. There is now wide recognition that the mass strength of union membership is a crucial resource in any political initiative, whether in the Commons or outside. George Woodcock once said, when he was General Secretary of the TUC: 'We have left Trafalgar Square, we are now in the corridors of power'. But it's no good being in that corridor on your own! A representative of the labour movement needs the visible presence and support of one hundred—two hundred—thousand workers in Trafalgar Square. The trade unions have to keep relearning this lesson, and the experience of the past two years or so has done a lot to drive it home.

As a general conclusion I can say that I am optimistic about the forward march of labour. It is not because I believe that a new round of easy pragmatic gains like those of the fifties and early sixties is in view. There is no doubt in my mind that the more successful we are, the greater the political conflict will be. If we elect a Labour government on the sort of terms I want, there is no question of a passive acceptance of its programme by the kind of people I've spent my life fighting against. They will perceive the implications of such a programme and will do all in their power to resist it. But the terms of that programme are now emerging, in policy declarations by the Labour Party conference and in constitutional changes ensuring that those declarations will become the firm commitments of the next Labour government.

Hilary Wainwright

One of the main purposes of Eric Hobsbawm's article is to alert us to the political limits of post-war trade union militancy in Britain.[1] It is impossible to deny the existence of such limits when, after twenty years of aggressive trade unionism, the vast majority of working-class people elect the most reactionary political regime in post-war history; but Hobsbawm's analysis of the nature of these limits is unconvincing. He explains the weaknesses of modern trade unionism mainly in the sociological terms of sectional divisions between different groups of workers. I will question the empirical basis for this emphasis; and then go on to place more explanatory emphasis on the failings, in the face of capitalist crisis, of the political map that has traditionally guided the march of labour. This map has led trade unionism into particularly narrow paths in which the unions are unable to use their considerable power to meet social needs that have grown rapidly as the boom—and with it the reforms of social democracy—has collapsed. The result has been a strengthening of divisions that Hobsbawm hardly mentions: between the trade unions and those whose needs lie beyond the employment contract, such as the young unemployed, women, and male workers in aspects of their lives not covered by the wage bargain. The marchers are, therefore, regrouping—both inside and outside the trade unions.

Consider first, the most obvious example of where an investig-

[1] Thanks to Roy Bhaskar, Bob Fryer and Sheila Rowbotham for helpful comments on the first draft of this article.

ation of the difficulties facing the politics of British trade unionism would provide a far more adequate explanation of the limits of trade union militancy than a sweeping sociological generalization. Hobsbawm asserts that workers' increased bargaining power has led to a new divisiveness between different groups of workers. It is perfectly true that wage claims have been going far beyond calculations of custom or traditional notions of a 'fair day's pay'. But the strength of the bargaining power behind the claims is usually dependent on the cohesion of workers' organizations. The success of these higher claims has depended on effective coordination among all those groups of workers, including those in different unions or workplaces, directly or indirectly affected by the dispute. From the fifties onwards, as trade unionists became aware of their potential bargaining power, (initially in the motor industry and parts of engineering), they began to extend their workplace organization to realize this potential. Thus, the last thirty years, far from seeing growing divisions, have, at a workplace level, seen the growth of greater contact and coordination.

In manufacturing, the number of shop stewards committees bringing together all manual unions on a particular site has been steadily increasing. Moreover, in the last four or five years the growth of white collar trade unionism has led to increased cooperation between shop floor and staff representatives. A recent survey of 1,000 manufacturing establishments of fifty employees or more (covering every major manufacturing classification) reports that joint manual shop stewards organizations exist in 52 per cent of the establishments, and staff and shop floor union 'work closely together' in 54 per cent. By contrast, when research into shop floor organizations and white-collar trade unionism was being carried out for the Donovan commission, close contact between staff and hourly-paid workers was so rare as to be not worth a mention.

Shop stewards' coordination across workplaces within one company (shop stewards' combine committees) has also grown since the time of the Donovan research, which reported that 12 per cent of stewards in a survey of about 1,500 were involved in some form of multi-union combine committee. In the more recent survey joint shop stewards' combine committees existed in 53 per cent of companies organizing bargaining at a group or divisional level. Even in companies where the most important level of bargaining was at the workplace itself, 29 per cent of the shop stewards' committees felt that coordination was important enough to organize on a multi-site as well as multi-union level.[2]

By stressing these trends away from sectionalism I do not want to imply that all is well on the shop floor. Clearly the weakness of trade-union resistance to the spate of redundancies from 1974 onwards indicates that the trends towards greater coordination are not sufficient to counter the pressures of the recession. The problem, however, has little to do with the militancy of one section threatening the interests of another. It has more to do with the reluctance of trade-union organizations to devise policies that challenge investment decisions; that reject the criteria of markets and production requirements of profit, and that spell out how production could be organized to meet social needs. Such political reflexes as did exist within the trade unions have become thoroughly sclerotic through the practice of abrogating all responsibility for social reorganization in favour of the Labour Party and the existing state machinery. Few of the new shop-floor-based organizations that developed in the fifties and sixties did anything to tone up these reflexes. But those that did, for example in Lucas Aerospace and in the power engineering industry, have been the only organizations able to develop alternative policies for their industries and to generate the strength to resist redundancies.[3]

Hobsbawm's arguments about divisions caused by strikes in the public sector can be countered in a similar way. Again, there is little evidence for his sweeping generalization that a major *new* source of division has been opened up by the increased role of the state as an employer and the disruptive tactics used by state employees to put pressure on governments. First, the

[2] W. Brown, ed., *The Changing Contours of British Industrial Relations*, Oxford 1981.

[3] See *State Intervention in Industry: a Workers' Inquiry*, Coventry, Liverpool, Newcastle and North Tyneside Trades Councils, for the history of these two campaigns.

inconvenience caused to working people in general by one group of workers going on strike is nothing peculiar to the last thirty years. The increased role of the state as an employer and provider of services perhaps makes this inconvenience more obvious and more concentrated. But strikes of bus workers, of dockers, and miners have always deprived the public directly or indirectly of commodities and services. This is a result of the fact that markets and commodities constitute the links between workers and those who have need of the use values they produce or provide. Secondly, even if we accept that there is an increase in the potential for divisions, the relationship between inconvenience caused and solidarity lost is not as straightforward as Hobsbawm implies. The extent to which workers are divided as a result of such public sector strikes depends on how far people blame the workers for the inconvenience, rather than feeling the government should have met their demands. For instance, opinion polls conducted during both the 1972 and 1974 miners' strikes indicated that while over 60 per cent considered that strikes were the major problem facing the government, over 55 per cent expressed sympathy with the miners. This would seem to show that there can be variations in the apportioning of responsibility for the inconvenience; depending on what group of workers is concerned, on the past record of support given by those workers to others, the strength of their case, how far the strikers try to regulate the inconvenience caused and so on.

However, all this is not to deny that workers in the public sector, the welfare sector especially, do face a problem in taking strike action, because of the direct relation of their work to people's needs. The models of militancy they inherit from traditional trade unionism in the manufacturing sector have proved to be inadequate. As a result, public sector workers are developing a new kind of trade unionism that takes more account of the relation of these workers to the wider working-class community. In some recent wage struggles in the public sector there has been a much stronger workers' control element than in most strikes in the private manufacturing sector. For example, during the civil servants' 1979 pay dispute the unions did not organize a general, undiscriminating strike of their members. Rather, they targeted areas where strike action would cause maximum inconvenience to the government and a minimum to the public. The unions tried to make sure that their activity did not disrupt pension and benefits payments. Similar tactics were used in some areas during the health workers' strike of that year. In Liverpool, the ancillary staff unions negotiated and then monitored an agreement with the Area Health Authority at the beginning of the strike, whereby specified essential services would be provided so long as standard pay was not reduced (even though not all duties were being performed) and so long as no volunteers were brought in. In struggles over hospital closures—for example, at Hounslow, Elizabeth Garrett Anderson, St. Benedict's, Bethnal Green, Brent—groups in the wider community needing and using the hospitals have been much more directly involved than in most factory-based redundancy struggles. Moreover, demands and discussions about the running of the hospital, the needs it meets and how adequately, what kind of hospital the users and the workers want, have become central to many campaigns against cuts and closures.

These developments are as yet fragile and sporadic, but they are an attempt to overcome the weaknesses of traditional trade-union and labour-movement politics—weaknesses that have paradoxically become more damaging as the crisis facing British capitalism deepens. The problem lies in the failure of the trade unions to express the wider needs of working class people. This failure is reflected in the widespread hostility felt towards the trade union movement, and in the deep division, not so much between different grades or groups of workers, but between, for instance, employed workers and the young unemployed, between male trade unionists and all but the most organized groups of women, and between workers as trade unionists and working-class people as consumers and users of services. To explain these failures and divisions we need to look at the consequences of British trade-union practice in the face of capitalist crisis and recession.

British trade unionism, more than any other major European trade union movement, limits itself to fighting for the interests of the wage earners, full stop. The assumption, and to some extent the practice, underlying this self-restriction is that all the worker's other needs, as a sick person, as a mother or father, as a pensioner, a traveller, a tenant, a black person fighting racism, and a citizen with a desire for peace, are met by helping the Labour Party gain control of the state, nationally and locally. What then are the consequences of this combination in a period when British employers are in a weak competitive position and when increased state expenditure in a mixed economy further fuels inflation? And, in this context, how has the labour movement become increasingly isolated? Let us consider the following two elements of trade union policy, and their effects on the attitudes of groups within the wider working class community.

1. Though unemployment is continuing to rise, trade unions more often than not still press for maximum overtime; and in response to threatened redundancies the priority of negotiators is normally to secure large payments for voluntary redundancies. The reduction of unemployment levels is, it is assumed by national trade union leaders, primarily a matter for government action, involving pressure on the Tories or the right commitments from the Labour Party. However, the traditional instruments of state intervention and expenditure, in the hands of a Labour government, have proved unable to reduce unemployment without increasing inflation, leading to more unemployment. The result of this combination of narrow trade unionism and failed state intervention, over time, has been a gradual distancing from the labour movement of not only the long-term unemployed, but especially the young unemployed, young people generally, and those such as teachers, parents and others who feel concerned about the bleak future facing these young people.

2. Although the needs to be met by the welfare state have greatly expanded, particularly as a result of the massive increase in the number of women who go out to work, the trade unions take little active interest in whether or not these needs are actually being met. Several trade unions have passed well

intentioned conference resolutions concerning, for example, better nursery provision, more expenditure on the NHS, better state care for old people and for the mentally ill, and other social responsibilities that used to be borne by women unpaid, at home. But such resolutions are merely passed on to the Labour Party for possible government action. They are not seen as the basis for trade-union campaigning and industrial pressure, especially when it is the Labour Party which fails to carry them out. During the fifties and early sixties, when social provision was expanding, these self-imposed limits in no way weakened the position of trade unions. The partnership with the Labour Party worked to the benefit of trade-union credibility. But once Labour governments could no longer meet these growing social needs and expectations, the unions were left in the cold, like emperors without their clothes. Their power was revealed for what it simply was: the capacity to bargain over the employment contract. As such it has been resented by those whose needs are wider than that. The narrow objectives of most trade-union militancy have made it easy for governments to find a scapegoat for their own failure to meet wider social needs. This relationship between attitudes towards trade unions and the flow of social provision and jobs explains the paradox that resentment towards trade-union power has in fact grown in the years when that power has declined, due to growing unemployment.

This analysis would date the first slowing down of the march of labour in its traditional direction to the second Wilson government and the beginning of the recession. This is, in fact, when the first indications of declining support began to appear in terms of a steady decline in the Labour vote and increased hostility towards the unions. The tremendous show of trade-union militancy in the early seventies, with all its political overtones, does not invalidate this analysis. For, in contrast with Hobsbawm's analysis, my focus is not on any weakness in the actions that trade unions *do* take. The focus of my explanation is rather on what the trade unions have *not* done and their failure to be political in the sense of campaigning around the wider social needs of working-class people and other oppressed groups. It is a failure built in to the partnership that makes up the labour movement in Britain; and it only began to undermine the movement when the political side of the partnership failed to meet its commitments.

This analysis points not only to the forces halting the march of labour but also to the impetus behind explorations of new directions. For many politically conscious trade unionists are aware of the absences that have allowed the labour movement to become increasingly isolated, now that parliamentary socialism can no longer provide a cover. And these trade unionists, unlike those of the thirties, face the recession with their workplace organizations intact. Again, unlike an earlier generation, they have been too disillusioned by the experience of majority Labour governments to leave politics entirely to the Labour Party. Finally, over the last ten years or so, there has been strong pressure and vigorous criticism from movements fighting around the very social needs that trade unionism has ignored. The numerous groups and campaigns that have together created the women's movement have been the most sustained critics and sources of pressure. Tenants' groups, anti-racist groups, organizations of the unemployed, environmental and anti-nuclear groups, among others, have also tried to involve local trade union organizations in their campaigns. The result of all this has been a growing trend for workplace and local trade-union organizations—shop stewards' committees and trades councils for instance—to take unprecedently wide-ranging initiatives on social and political issues.

At this point I can do little more than list some examples. What they have in common is that in all sorts of *ad hoc* ways they are filling the vacuum left by the collapse of the traditional combination of parliamentary socialism and economistic trade unionism. What they have positively in common has yet to be formulated. A list of examples includes the growth of campaigns around cuts in public expenditure involving community-based groups of women and unemployed as well as trade unionists, and which raise issues concerning the quality, content, and control of social provision, as well as its amount. Similarly, several industrial shop stewards' committees, the best-known being the Lucas Aerospace shop stewards' committee, have moved away from the traditional emphasis on the extent of state intervention and investment towards questioning the purpose of state and private investment in a capitalist economy. They have fought for their own workers' plans for production and investment according to social needs. This has led them to create links with groups campaigning for better health and transport facilities and for non-nuclear energy programmes. In less dramatic ways, shop stewards' committees taking action to control the introduction of new technology, to protect the health and safety of workers and the wider community, are also questioning the purpose of investment, and taking action to control it. Tenants' groups in Wales, the North East, Coventry and elsewhere, with the support of UCATT branches and several trades councils have been taking direct action too, to control the decisions which effect them. Many of these tenants' groups are led by women, sensing for the first time the strength of collective action. The list could go on, depending on where you live and what your main political involvements are. Moreover, many of these organizations are developing their own national structures and networks of contact: the Joint Forum of Combine Committees, the National Housing Liaison Committee, the Network of Trade Union and Community Resource Centres, and more.

As yet these developments have no adequate political expression. But the struggles within the Labour Party partially reflect the emergence of this new kind of socialist politics. For instance, the demand for accountability of MPs and the party leader, is for many of those who support the Labour left, not just about inner-party democracy. It is also about what kind of a party can successfully challenge the non-parliamentary forces of capitalist bureaucracy and wealth. The demand for accountability to the labour movement outside parliament is, for some, an assertion that it is outside parliament that labour's real social and economic power lies, even if we need a parliamentary expression of that power.

The new directions that socialist and trade-union politics is taking do not, however, find direct or adequate expression and scope for development in this struggle inside the Labour Party. For that struggle remains constrained by the traditional partnership of narrow trade unionism and parliamentary socialist illusions. Only when the limits on change within the Labour Party become clear and the new political trade unionism of recent years breaks free of this partnership, can we hope to overcome the deep popular indifference and hostility that have halted the march of labour.

Jack Adams

One of my earliest childhood political memories is of the Black Country council elections in 1946. The local Labour candidate's election address reflected the confidence of working people that, having defeated fascism, we were going to build socialism. Compared with Labour's 1979 manifesto, it makes stirring reading:

'During the past six years, Black Country men and women in common with their brothers and sisters throughout Britain have been engaged in the colossal task of breaking the military might of the most reactionary regime known to man. The fascist enemy has been laid low. The task is not ended.

'We now enter the most progressive period in British politics. Great opportunities await us, if we grasp them our lives can be fuller and freer than ever before.

'Opportunities are only opportunities unless we organize now to meet the needs of our people. Every constituent *must* be involved. Have you insisted that *your* local Council consult *you* on what you require for your community?

'Remember: it is your business—you must help decide how and in what environment you wish to live—that is democracy. You fought for it.

'Why not a people's plan and policy for the Black Country?

'Industry; Education; Health; Homes; Environment; these are all democratic issues that concern us all, working for a socialist Black Country. Get involved in your politics.'

The candidate won by a landslide. The following three-and-a-half decades have brought the labour movement both achievements and disappointment, but, taken as a general proposition, Eric Hobsbawm's overall analysis seems to me valid. If not halted, the advance has certainly been checked.

This is not to say that there have been no positive landmarks. On the contrary, to cite only two examples, there can be no doubt that the magnificent mobilization against the Industrial Relations Act and the miners' defeat of the Heath government were tremendous achievements. However, mass support for political advance and the assertion of class consciousness in struggle seem to have waned throughout the period highlighted by Hobsbawm. My conclusions are based not on the statistics of declining Labour Party votes and membership but on experience among trade unionists at factory level and in canvassing for the Communist Party and the Labour Party. Among elderly people I frequently find a sympathetic response and a clear class understanding in discussion. These are less strong in later generations, although many young people are evidently looking for a radical alternative.

Why has the forward march of labour been checked? Hobsbawm presents several arguments here, but there are two major omissions in the case he outlines: first, the role of the mass media; and second, the consistent strategic attacks on the organized labour movement from the late sixties onwards.

The almost exclusive control of newspapers by big capitalist enterprises is a very powerful weapon for the British ruling class. Fleet Street and its local counterparts—like the *Birmingham Evening Mail*, which we at Leyland have to deal with—are very effective propaganda machines. They regularly oppose workers involved in disputes—the firemen in 1977, the public sector workers in their fight against Callaghan's 5 per cent pay policy, and many more. On occasion—say, the TUC Day of Action or the sacking of Derek Robinson at Leyland—their coverage is simply scandalous. This bias is not reserved for industrial disputes. There is an endless flow of propaganda knocking the nationalized industries, calling them wasteful and inefficient, caricaturing socialism as bureaucratic and hostile to individuality, and asserting that only the free market can produce the wealth and prosperity on which our social services depend. Lies, distortions and half-truths are all mixed together in constant denigration of the left and the trade union movement. There is no doubt that Thatcher's right-wing radicalism appealed to many who were conditioned by this daily diet, especially the young working-class voters. When Thatcher claimed that one of her major achievements was to have changed people's attitudes, she did less than full justice to the role her Fleet Street allies had played.

A main aim of the media has been to undermine the campaigning ability of the trade union and other democratic movements. We must not underestimate the major offensive that the ruling class has undertaken in its efforts to neutralize the trade unions in particular. There have been many different kinds of measure, but their common purpose has been to regulate extra-parliamentary activity and weaken the unions' ability to act in defence of their members and for wider social change. Some of these measures we were able to resist, among them the Labour and Tory legislation against the unions in the late sixties and early seventies. We now have to make sure that James Prior's Employment Act meets equally effective resistance. Other measures like the Redundancy Payments Act were welcomed by some at the time but have turned out to have serious negative effects. The redundancy legislation in particular has disrupted the fight for jobs and greased the wheels for mass unemployment.

One area singled out for special attention is that of the joint shop stewards' and combine committees. These have been among the most important features of working-class organization and politics since the Second World War. Shop stewards' committees are the most effective answer to sectionalism on the shop floor, and combines have helped bring unity to separate factories facing the same employer. The press and Tory industrial relations 'experts' reserve their fiercest attacks for shop stewards and convenors. They fear shop-floor democracy more than anything else. In this light we can see how serious a setback for the whole working class was the sacking of Derek

Robinson, then chairman of the British Leyland Combine Committee, when he tried to present an alternative to the Edwardes plan for cutbacks and redundancies. Robinson's victimization was a symbolic intimidation of working-class leaders who dare to resist the offensive and pose alternatives. (Incidentally, these attacks on joint shop stewards' and combine committees cast interesting light on Hobsbawm's estimate of the danger of sectionalism, which I do not share. In recent years there has been a greater degree of united action than I have ever known before. This has been my experience at different levels of the trade union movement. Of course, many sectional problems remain, but when I recall the situation described by Harry Pollitt in his *Serving My Time*, I think it wrong to argue that sectionalism is on the increase.)

When considering the present situation of the labour movement, we must recognize the negative role of the mass media and the persistent attacks of the ruling class on our movement. But in the final analysis, it is the lack of political, class understanding that has allowed some of these attacks to succeed, leaving us facing the most vicious Conservative government for half a century. We are now in a new situation. The policies of the postwar boom are no longer applicable. The Tories under Thatcher have grasped an opportunity created by the social-democratic socialism of Wilson and Callaghan. They have filled the political vacuum and moved politics to the right. The question facing us all now is: how can we remove this government and resume the forward march of labour?

This will not be easy, but it can be done if we learn from our experience. The main answer to the stagnation that seems to hold back the movement at the moment must be a broad-based, politically conscious class movement with a vision of socialism that masses of people can identify with. The organized working class is vital here, as the 'Establishment' sometimes seems to recognize better than we do. Of course the left has suffered major setbacks in some unions, notably the AUEW, but there are hopeful signs that Labour's rank and file are asserting themselves against the Party's right wing. However, there is a lesson from the past that can be learned here. We must remember to distinguish between what happens at the Labour Party Conference and what is happening among the masses. In retrospect, I think we attach a great deal of importance to major political events—like the battle of Saltley Gates, say—but too readily assume that they express a similar degree of mass political consciousness among workers generally.

Today, if we conduct large-scale mass campaigns on issues such as jobs, I think there are big opportunities for increasing support for socialist politics, with the working class at the centre of the broad-based movement we need to build. In the past few years, we have seen positive developments, with the trade unions widening their horizons and activity. The growing interest in working out alternative plans and in health and safety are two examples of our movement seeking to influence the production process. The movement is also reaching out to others. There is now a lot more understanding of the women's movement. The actions against the Corrie Bill restricting abortion proved that people are responsive to issues based on principle. The revival of the peace movement is very encouraging. A whole new generation, especially the young, is finding it possible to unite around the goals of peace and disarmament. Also there are important changes in the Labour Party. Although the victories of the left do not mean that a revitalized, federal party of the working class is just around the corner, they do point to the activists' understanding that there must be a break with the Labour Party 'socialism' of the past three decades.

The experience of Thatcherism may provide the springboard for real democratic advance, if only we can make realistic analyses of our prospects. There is no shortage of issues on which to fight: education, women's rights, peace, a new economic strategy, trade union rights, social services, health, anti-racism. These are all issues that can be fought in a non-sectarian way by a mass movement with viable alternative policies. What is clear, though, is that none of this can be done on the basis of consensual, 'moderate', Social Contract–style policies. It will require a massive ideological offensive that points to the vision of socialism that I got through *The British Road to Socialism*.

Raymond Williams

If it were only a halt in a forward march it would all be very much simpler. People take these figures of speech to make discussion more lively, but the figure of a 'forward march' is from an antiquated kind of military campaign based on the poor bloody infantry. Its only contemporary use is in parade-ground exercises, with sergeant majors bawling their orders. And actually one of these orders is 'Halt!'—to get new orders, to reorganize, to have a bit of a rest. There must still be some people, including some in what is called the leadership, who really do see contemporary politics like this.

The rest of us cannot afford to. What was plain to some from the beginning, and what for very many is now slowly sinking in, is that we have recently lived through a major defeat. We should not hide behind figures of speech. The defeat has happened, and its extent is formidable. Who among us could have believed in 1945 or 1966, or even in 1974, that at the beginning of the 1980s we should have not only a powerful right-wing government, trying with some success to go back to the politics and the economics of the 1930s, but—even worse—a social order that has literally decimated the British working class, imposing the cruelty of several million unemployed?

That figured in nobody's perspectives of a forward march. Now that it has happened it has to be faced in its real terms. Eric Hobsbawm faced some of it in 1978. But because he faced it, not in the easy habit of projection—'take two deep breaths, spit and say "Thatcher" '—but in the harder spirit of looking at our own organizations, assumptions and ideas, to see how it could be that such openly reactionary forces could, even temporarily, defeat us, he got, from some, little thanks. Ritual spitting, ritual reassurance ('you just wait till next time'), are so much easier to go in for.

He wouldn't claim to have got all the analysis right, but what he said is still a good place to start. I'd come in, first, on an underlying point. To what extent, after the experience of these years, can we still talk, realistically, of a single entity called 'the labour movement'? Most of us know, with Hobsbawm, why our forecasts called it and served it as a *movement*. It was a coming together, under hard conditions, to help each other, to connect immediate struggles, to move through and beyond them to change society. It was a movement rather than just another institution. It organized, but to extend the movement rather than just to sustain an organization.

Of course we must then also say that as it became more successful it made many institutions, was recognized as a set of institutions in modern society, had large and complex organizations to keep going. That is both a fact and a problem. For into these changed conditions the imagery if not always the reality of a movement persisted. There is one strange image that we all grew up with: that of the industrial and political *wings*. Wings of what? Of a bird, of an aeroplane? But then what happens if one of the wings starts seeing itself as 'the natural governing party' in a still predominantly capitalist social order; indeed as independent and autonomous in the sovereignty of parliament? And what happens, further, if the other wing, for its own reasons, starts flapping in the opposite direction? In a bird or an aeroplane that is the moment of nosedive, and you would expect to hear the noise of mutual recriminations on the way down to the crash. Wings? But then where is the body, where is the head? In the period since 1945 we have not faced these underlying problems. Instead we keep saying that the wings must maintain regular contact, must take care to fly together and at the same speed, must flap steadily on to their undoubted common destinations. But that is what now needs questioning. Do these wings, as they now are, even belong to the same body?

In the crudest sense, yes. They are at once the historical

creation and the still major organized embodiment of British working people. Everything that Hobsbawm says about the conditions of this creation and embodiment, but also about the really major subsequent changes in social conditions—in part as a result of their success—seems to me to be true. But does he sufficiently distinguish between the effects of the changes on what can still in some ways be seen as a whole movement, and the more differentiated effects on specific elements of the movement and indeed on what have now become, in many respects, independent and largely self-referring institutions?

Consider first the differential effects on trade unions. The factors that Hobsbawm analyses are all historical realities, and so far from being capable of being reversed are in many cases, because of radical changes in the labour processes themselves, virtually certain to intensify. And that they have led to the dominance of certain political tendencies, to the practical habits of what he calls sectionalism and economism, is equally evident.

But we have to pull back beyond this, for on its own it can lead only too quickly to mutual recrimination during the nosedive. Some years ago I described one of the same phenomena as 'militant particularism'; an awkward phrase, but I wanted to get past my simple equation of militancy with *socialism*. Of course almost all labour struggles begin as particularist. People recognize some condition and problem they have in common, and make the effort to work together to change or solve it. But then this is nothing special in the working class. You have only to look at the militancy of stockbrokers or of country landowners or of public-school headmasters. The unique and extraordinary character of working-class self-organization has been that it has tried to connect particular struggles to a general struggle in one quite special way. It has set out, as a movement, to make real what is at first sight the extraordinary claim that the defence and advancement of certain particular interests, properly brought together, are in fact in the general interest. That, after all, is the moment of transition to an idea of socialism. And this moment comes not once and for all but many times; is lost and is found again; has to be affirmed and developed, continually, if it is to stay real.

You can say it was idealism that led to that moment: the vision of a better society. You can say that it was hard bitter learning: that you would lose or only ever partly win particular struggles unless you could generalize and broaden them, and change their underlying conditions. In history, and today, there is plenty of both. But what has to be faced now, honestly and without recrimination, is that the struggle for that moment—the moment of transition to the *idea* of socialism quite as much as of a transition to socialist practice—has been at least temporarily lost. This is so not only in the fact that we have been defeated at the most general level—it is reasonable to argue that we can recover from that. The point is that the struggle has been to an important extent lost inside our own organizations, and that no amount of necessary and militant defence or advancement of our own particular interests will of itself recover it. Indeed the most shattering fact in our culture is that not only the employers and the rich and their friends and agents believe and say that we are all interested only in selfish advantage: a *majority* in our society believe and say this, including a large and growing number, cynically or angrily, within our own organizations.

Well, it has been said before. We know boss-class propaganda when we hear it. Breathe twice and spit. But it is genuinely more serious than that. Within the culture of poverty, from which by struggle and organization our forebears led so many of us, the claim that these particular interests amounted to a general interest had a certain absolute cast. It could not be right for so many human beings to live like that. So no matter what those very poor and hard-driven men and women were actually thinking, even if they had nothing in mind but some temporary easement, they were in a certain absolute sense right. In fact, even in the hardest times, some of them were thinking much further. It is often still so today. It has been true, in recent struggles, of the local authority manual workers, of the miners, of the nurses: particular claims and true general interests.

But it can no longer be taken for granted that so absolute a link is inevitably present, and certainly not that it is magically conferred by the fact that it is a trade union action. Just because, with such good other effects, unionism has developed within relatively comfortable, even relatively privileged white-collar and even professional occupations, the older absolute ratification based on poverty and exposure is no longer there. It is then much more a case of the busy bargaining of interest groups; is seen like that, most of the time, from inside; is almost always seen like that from outside, including by many of the other interest groups. It is indeed, in prevailing conditions, a necessary process. It is part of the mechanism of a modern capitalist society. Even most modern capitalists want only to regulate it, and to steer it away from more dangerous ideas like changing the social order or going beyond the mere bargaining process to direct action.

This is the point at which we can see what has so widely happened. Other much more powerful interest groups, in the state, in the city, in the big corporations, are still there, combining, and the rest of us say: 'while they do it, we do it'. But they are not the only people beyond us. There are the millions of marginal and beyond-the-margin poor in our own country but also in far greater numbers in many very poor countries with which we trade. The indifference of modern capitalism to all those who live beyond the current bargaining terms and procedures is well known and shameful. But the question then is: do we join that indifference, or do we really try to surpass it?

This is again the moment of socialism: a moment that is more than some verbal affiliation. It is the moment when we have to show, not only to our own satisfaction, which is usually easy, but to an effective majority of others, which is very much harder, that our particular interests promote, are compatible with, or at least do not damage, the general interest. And then it is necessary to recognize that within the terms of ordinary bargaining—the everyday mechanisms of a capitalist labour market—this is only rarely certain to be the case. Indeed it is only the bourgeoisie that has ever tried to believe it: that pursuing special interests ensures the general interest, by a hidden hand. It was the whole mean, false and privileged view of society that first the labour movement, and then more consciously and more effectively the socialist movement, set out to challenge, to destroy, but above all, *to replace*. What we are then saying is that trade unions on their own, acting only as trade unions, cannot change the social order and make a new kind of society. But as they get more powerful they can mitigate its effects, make some changes *inside* it, and in the end even make the existing order relatively unworkable. All this has been happening, but within it, for generations much more has been seen and attempted. That was the political effort: founding and funding the Labour Party; seeing it as the way to a new social order.

What Hobsbawm says about the modern Labour Party, and about what I suppose we must still, with an effort, call the Labour Party's governments, seems to me true but very restrained. The process has been an uneven one, and so it's hard to put a date to. But, on the one hand (the one wing), it's been clear for a long time that the Labour Party in parliament has had no intention of changing the social order, though it has made some important reforms inside it. And in the same period, the trade union movement has not really been pressing them to do anything of the kind, though it has supported the reforms and has insisted on particular measures important to the unions as such. This recrimination between the wings is relatively pointless. The timing may often have gone wrong, many details have been argued about, but the long slow flap has been broadly in a common direction: towards what seemed a reasonable future, which we might all have settled for, but which has now, rather suddenly, been cancelled.

This is the present crisis. This is what is wrong with all those ideas of a simple forward march. The underlying perspectives of a reforming Labour Party and of a steadily bargaining and self-improving trade-union movement—a perspective within which so many major gains have been achieved—suddenly look like and are dead ends.

I have then no doubt that, as in every previous period of major change in world history, most existing leaders, still confident inside their powerfully established institutions, will fight like the devil to keep the old perspectives, the old methods, alive.

What else, after all, can most of them practically do? It has been, as they say, their whole lives. But then what has happened before is not that the old leaders change, or even that they are quickly replaced by new leaders, with new ideas and new methods. What usually happens first, and it can take a long time, is that the old institutions go on being outwardly powerful and impressive, while they wither from inside: their membership stagnant or declining; full of faction and manoeuvre; a slowly settling mood of resignation and cynicism, since nothing quite works any longer, in the old ways, though inside the institutions most experienced people still say that any new ways are quite impractical. This seems to me the evident condition today of large parts of the Labour Party and of the trade-union movement. Of course, in these circumstances, nobody will be thanked for saying so.

But then what is this so-called major change in world history? Isn't it just (spit) Thatcher, or (spit) Wilson, or (spit) whoever? If that were only so! There is indeed a specific crisis of *British* capitalism, with many special local features. But this crisis has occured within the massive penetration of British capitalism by a more powerful international (including British) capitalism, and by the politics and culture of an imperialist military and political alliance. Moreover, what we now face is that wider system itself in crisis, amid the powerful consequences of a world-wide movement against imperialism. This has happened in poor countries, determined at last to make their own history. They are trying to advance their particular interests, from within their poverty, as both particular and general human interests. It has happened with much more effect in other, strategically rich countries, able to disturb and permanently alter some of the terms of trade, and thus to shift and threaten to overthrow the general conditions within which those old local bargains were struck. Furthermore, all this is happening within the deadly military confrontation between the imperialist alliance and now powerfully established socialist states, most of these new states not of our own kind of foreseeing or desire. And then, most profoundly underlying these different levels of crisis, there is the newly realized and decisive fact: that we cannot *materially* go on in the old ways; that at key points in our modern labour processes, and especially in inputs of energy, there will be at best radical limitation, at worst absolute shortages, within which, while we stick to the old terms, we shall be able only to scramble and fight for some temporary advantage.

Well, we all know all that. Or do we? On television or in the papers some of us know it. But nobody really knows it until it has been tracked back into everyday life. So we are penetrated by international capitalism? All right, get out (spit) of the Common Market, or put on import controls. But while anybody's even talking about proposals like that, the real world is moving. For capital can pick up and move much faster than any worker. Jobs can be rapidly transferred to where the labour is cheaper or less organized. British capital, to cut its costs and to restore its rate of profit, can move overnight to some flag of convenience. Yet still the rest of us are here, on an island crowded by the success of that now vanishing (vanished?) position of priority and privilege in the world. So shall we become more productive, more efficient? Let British capitalism modernize itself. But at *our* expense? By renegotiating the rate of profit, which over the years, by organization, we have steadily reduced? Not likely, even when the flags of convenience are flying all around us, and the international corporations are getting ready to wave goodbye.

This is the moment of the differential effect. The Labour Party in parliament, taking some of this crisis on board, forgets any new social order, settles for a hopefully new nationalism, finds ways of trying to modernize British capitalism from the public revenue. It is then opposed not only by those who do not want to pay taxes to raise the revenue. Not only by those 'consumers'— and we are all consumers now—who, consulting their particular interests and finding their calculations satisfactory, decide that they 'have no alternative' but to buy foreign manufactures. So watch it with this talk of import controls. But centrally, and critically, opposed by the trade union movement, on its own most necessary ground. For while the process is only the modernization of British *capitalism*, and of analogous state enterprises, it is at every level, from restoring the rate of profit to what is called 'productivity' (which is nearly always, in practice, getting the same output with fewer workers—and, in the necessary new processes, millions fewer, acting against the established and both short and long-term interests of the working class as a whole.

It's relatively easy, intellectually, when it is the current sort of fight against a Tory government. But during most of the years since 1966 there has been a more shattering inner history: a fight, with truces and with fragile compromises, between essential working-class interests and this now quite separate political programme. And we can't just say that, when we have spat out Thatcher, in fantasy or—with much more difficulty— in fact, we can simply go on as before, in some old perspective. An underlying unity, of interest and purpose, may still survive, subjectively, in minds. It is honoured in memory and still often active in aspiration. But objectively that unity has gone, or is very rapidly going. And this is the profound reason for the crises, the differential crises, within the labour movement, which Hobsbawm began to describe.

Yet is that, miserably, the end of the story? It certainly could be, unless we are very open and honest with each other, and start to do some new kinds of work. Perhaps what will happen is that the British trade-union movement will indeed accommodate, radically, to a Labour government of this type, or to some more openly centrist government. The American, the recent German, the Japanese solution? It would gain some temporary advantages, for an even smaller number of people, but of course that would be the end of the historical labour movement. Yet if not accommodation, will it then be defeat, lasting rather than temporary defeat? That too is possible, if the crisis deepens still further, and if the much more authoritarian solutions that are already being thought about are put into drastic action, isolating and controlling and finally emasculating the unions, with public opinion (already not exactly loath) readily mobilized against them? It couldn't happen here? Some steps in these directions are already well in hand.

So get ready for militant defence? Agreed. But as in most actions we shall need to do more than be defensive. We shall have really to establish, in this actual and rapidly-changing world rather than in any historical memory or rhetoric, a necessary and workable settlement between particular interests and the general interest. This will undoubtedly mean changing our minds, in many cases, about the form of our particular interests. And then, since it is bound to be painful, we have the unusually heavy duty—easy to say, very hard to discharge—of really making it equitable. We shall have to learn a whole new kind of negotiation, which the most lively parts of the movement are already approaching, trying to rethink our ideas of work and of the working life, and then as a crucial part of that, the realities rather than the habits of 'income' and 'wages'.

This will do much, but not enough. For what has really failed, inside the movement and inside the whole society, is any valid concept of the general interest. That is why appeals to it are so often resisted or rejected. In the forms in which we have known it—the undifferentiated 'nation', the needs of the 'economy'—it has again and again been a *false* general interest: a label stuck over a radically unequal society, or over a necessarily privileged and exploiting system. But while we have been talking about the failures of the labour movement, we ought to take note of one paradoxical kind of success. By sticking so tenaciously to particular interests, the falsehood of these versions of the general interest has been thoroughly demonstrated. Yet not consciously, not at the level of argument, only really at the level of feeling, of mood. Indeed it has been almost too thoroughly learned. One of the labour movement's central failings, since 1945, has been its quite insufficient attention to, and support of, research, education and popular argument. This failing has been especially painful in a period in which its own members and its own sons and daughters are in a very much better position to do such work. So that, lacking the necessary consciousness and argument, the falsehood of these versions of general interest has been demonstrated only in everyday practice, where they not only don't hold but are visibly not believed, even if everybody, on demand, can intone them, usually against other people.

That is a sort of success, for these versions of the needs of 'the nation' or 'the economy' are indeed in their usual forms false. But it is a dangerous sort of success, if all that is then left is the defence and advancement of particular interests, at a time when the earth is visibly shifting under us. There can be no reversion to those old forms, even at their most plausible. However it may be done, in the complexities of politics, and necessarily on a much wider than British scale, the concept of a practical and possible general interest, which really does include all reasonable particular interests, has to be negotiated, found, agreed, constructed.

It can only, I believe, be socialism. But not just the name, or some imported model. We can say that we must march in a different direction, towards a different kind of working democracy, gaining some real and equitable control over these terribly limiting objective conditions. That is indeed the right direction, but it will mean more than marching. It will mean rethinking, practically, every single one of our enterprises, and as part of this the relations between them. It will mean constructing, in convincing detail, from our shared practical experience and from tough intellectual analysis, the general shape of a new social order. Then, as we find agreements, it will mean uniting as far as we can to push through, against real opposition, to start to put it into effect, and probably again and again to amend it.

Wings? We have to put back the body. But the only body that will get anywhere will need a very clear head. So now, urgently, research, information, argument, publication: the conditions of any adequate militancy for a new kind of working class, a new and renewed labour *movement*.

Jack Jones

I don't basically disagree with Eric Hobsbawm's analysis and his response to the original discussion. Certainly the election of 1979 represented a major political set-back, particularly in the switch of Labour, including trade-unionist, votes to the Tories that we saw then. It is necessary here to note the populist, opportunist demagogy of the Tories, and the impact of this on working-class opinion—combined, of course, with a very right-wing press and increasing right-wing influence on television and radio, an influence that certainly had an effect in the Warrington by-election. The dangers of mass propaganda cannot be underestimated: it almost represents a new dimension in opinion-forming. In the United States it has already been used over many years against political labour, which in fact has almost been demolished; and now these techniques are being applied to render union power ineffective. They are a potential danger in Britain too, although I have the feeling that our shop stewards—a special feature of the British trade union movement—can ensure effective resistance. But even this is limited. In those undertakings where closures and redundancies are now occurring, employers when they start up again will try to forestall trade unionism of the militant kind, and we may well be in for a spate of sweetheart deals with union leaderships having no compunction or sense of trade-union principle.

Now, the original debate took place in 1979, and a lot has been written since then that looks remarkably foolish in retrospect—some of the contributions don't bear much examination. We must be careful to avoid a repetition of slogans and generalizations from the past, allied with a refusal to assess realistically the facts of the present. One salient fact of the present is that there is a mood of defeatism and a tendency to denigrate the reforms achieved by working-class struggle. At the same time, all of us must accept that there should by now have been greater advances towards a socialist society. How can these advances now be made? Concentrations of wealth and power, and social inequality, must be attacked, but in ways that workers see as being to their advantage. Simple campaigns around clearly defined, immediate political objectives must go alongside educational efforts to portray the benefits of socialism. One such campaign might be directed against the huge burden of defence expenditure, and it could be shown how the money involved could be diverted to socially useful purposes.

At the present time, we have a political leadership—I mean mainly Michael Foot and people close to him—that is prepared to fight both inside and outside Parliament. The Liverpool and Glasgow demonstrations and the People's March against unemployment were very successful, and more action of this kind is promised. Now, this is political action, and those who take part in it go through a tremendous educational experience. The trade unions are more willing than previously to participate in actions of this kind. The 1972 demonstration against the Industrial Relations Act represented a big turn in the attitude of union leaderships to mass demonstrations, and it had a unifying effect. The fact that political action of that kind was being taken by trade unionists certainly encouraged quite a number of union leaders to think of further such actions. That positive feature should be borne in mind when the general position is evaluated.

There certainly has been a halt in the forward march of labour, and this was apparent to me in the early seventies. From 1951 onwards, after the defeat of the Labour government, there had been a deepening division between the Labour Party leadership and the trade union movement—its rank and file at any rate—and this was mainly because the Labour leadership was not putting forward policies with much impact on working-class opinion. The leadership had the support of some trade union leaders, in terms of party finance and the block vote at Conference, but it had only a very weak relationship with the average individual member of the Labour Party or the average trade unionist. It was out of power for a long time, and didn't inspire much confidence. 1963–64 saw an attempted comeback, but still there was little understanding between the Party and the unions. There was some resurgence, but it was lost through the lack of commitment of Wilson, Jenkins, Brown and others in the new Labour government, through their inability to understand the need to put forward and carry out policies attractive to the working class. On the contrary, they persisted in very tight incomes policies and went on to *In Place of Strife*, which alienated rather than won the support of working people.

The disunity of the 1964–69 period, caused mainly by the Labour government's almost total disregard for trade-union views (except its retreat from *In Place of Strife*), was the reason for my proposals for a Liaison Committee of the TUC, the Parliamentary Party and the National Executive Committee of the Labour Party, and, second, a joint policy based on firm commitments, later to be called the Social Contract. One of the early items of policy-making was the document 'Economic Policy and the Cost of Living', which was a good starting point. It made possible some important advances by the unions: a lot of it was incorporated into Labour's 1974 election manifesto, and the Labour government, during its first period, acted on many of the manifesto's commitments. By and large, up to and including 1976, the government kept its word, and this because of its firm commitments to the trade union movement. We made progress on such things as the Health and Safety at Work Act, equal pay and limitations on racial discrimination. The introduction of the Employment Protection Act brought major improvements in the rights of workers. We also developed the social wage, with increased pensions linked to earnings and the introduction of child benefits. As a consequence of this, Labour was gaining a lot of respect and support in the workplaces in this period. The industrial committees of the TUC—a new development—were enhancing the unity of the movement on a national scale. Trade union membership grew. Shop stewards—a very important element that perhaps has not been sufficiently emphasized in the debate—grew in numbers. The Social Contract, following upon the united action and successes achieved in the fight against the Industrial Relations Act, for a time gave a sense of unity in the ranks. The failure to capitalize on this situation was a great misfortune brought about by a total withdrawal on the part of the Labour Party and the unions from strategic policy.

From 1977 onwards we indulged in the luxury of disunity. This was mainly the government's fault, but it meant that the influence of the unions on the government was weakened at a time when the government itself was weak. The unions should have tried to get the government to go to the electorate on a fightback programme at an early stage, rather than continue as a prisoner of the Liberals. But the whole situation deteriorated and led in the end to the disaster of 1979, primarily because of the government's insistence on the 5 per cent pay policy, but also because of the unions' failure to influence it towards an early election.

The most important purpose of a debate like this is to determine what needs to be done now. And what is lacking today are simple, clear, limited policies that workers can understand and fight for: demands to which the Labour leadership and the unions can be committed—and not just defensive demands, as in the case of the coal and steel industries, but aggressive ones around the issues of jobs, major public works schemes, housing construction plans, road development plans, in other words a big public expenditure programme. We need a realistic campaign for the 35-hour week, committing the politicians as well as the unions to a major effort; we need a campaign for increased pensions and child benefits, so that families too can be involved in the struggle. Campaigning against arms spending, for instance, we should not pose the simple demand of a reduction in the defence budget. The point would be to show that arms spending is increased to the detriment of the social wage, that the problems of pensioners, children and so on, the deficiencies of education and housing, are being aggravated by the diversion of resources into nuclear weapons. It would be a question of campaigning for improvements in social services as a priority, and in the course of this making clear that such improvements would entail a shift in public spending away from nuclear arms and towards areas of real popular need. It's not beyond the wit of the labour movements to publicize a campaign like this, to use television—for all its limitations—to develop poster campaigns, to place articles in a whole variety of newspapers, all in the effort to get the demands across.

In order to campaign effectively for such demands, of course, we need the united commitment of the entire labour movement, right from the top of the Labour Party and the unions down to the rank and file. Unity between the leadership of the unions and the rank and file is particularly vital. Where this is achieved, real progress can be made. The *de facto* defeat of the Industrial Relations Act was brought about by a combination of the top leadership, the shop stewards and the membership, and the successful struggle against *In Place of Strife* had the same united character. The demand for more jobs at a time of massive unemployment can strengthen the movement itself. It would help to win the black population to support for Labour and to a strong working-class political stance; a campaign for more jobs would earn more respect in black communities than the simple repetition of purely anti-racist slogans. More jobs is the answer to trade union weakness, and it is a political demand. At the moment, the left is weak and disunited, and, somehow, because much of the critical work now going on is of the academic intellectual variety, there is not much understanding among the trade-union rank and file about what has to be done. There has to be a complete reappraisal of how to enthuse the mass of trade unionists at a time when the movement is weakened by mass unemployment.

The fact now is that workers are retreating fast and the unions are tending to weaken. Regroupment is called for, based on a new, unified policy committing the Labour Party and the trade unions, strengthening the ranks and creating the confidence for the fight against unemployment and the huge cost of nuclear weapons, and for clear policies on the National Health

Service, more housing, expansion of public services, improved pensions and price control. Failure to produce a clear policy will mean reliance on a kind of anarchy. People tend to dream about revolution and think somehow that everything will happen automatically, that there will be a collapse of capitalism. But workers need to see and feel progress to gain confidence; they need an immediate cause to fight for. If the claims made by some of the contributors to the original debate had been borne out, we would be in a revolutionary situation by now. But we are far from that. For all its deficiencies, the idea of a Social Contract has a lot to recommend it. It means committing Labour's leaders to a definite immediate policy, and if the policy is the right one it can enthuse the ranks and give cohesion to what is now a disunited army.

I personally have always tried to fight for clearly defined demands, because that is the way to make progress with mass support inside and outside the trade unions. As I see it, the commitment of the Labour leadership, including Michael Foot, Tony Benn and Denis Healey, to a 35-hour week is more important than a commitment to a nationalization of twenty large companies. The first can command total support, because of the economic and technological factors that justify it, while the second may be regarded as unrealistic (in immediate terms) and safely left till later. You gain mass interest by fighting for things that people see as justified and feasible. The progress made to date is presently being reversed by strongly anti-working-class policies, including the display of Tory vengeance over the civil servants and British Leyland, the changes in the Employment Act, the repression of the trade union movement and, of course, mass unemployment. This is what we have to deal with. We are not just looking for theoretical justifications for our stances. We must find a way to recapture the unity of the labour movement and to secure a majority Labour government at the earliest opportunity.

Robin Blackburn

If the seventies ended badly for the left, both here and abroad, then the eighties have begun well enough to encourage us to discount the warnings implicit in Eric Hobsbawm's analysis. The advances of the left within the Labour Party, the growth in the activity and numbers of Party members, and the encouraging results of the local elections of May 1981 might be thought to represent a reversal of the trends that culminated in the debacle of the last Labour government and the consequent victory of Margaret Thatcher. Developments overseas—from Managua to Salisbury, from Gdansk to Paris—are a proper source of encouragement to those concerned with renewing the spirit and strength of the socialist and labour movement, even though, in each case, there are formidable problems and dangers to be confronted. Yet, however optimistically current events may be scanned, the 'pessimism of the intelligence' recommended by Eric Hobsbawm remains deeply salutary. Within the capitalist world generally, belligerent and reactionary forces are still gaining in strength; in Britain, capitalist crisis is imposing appalling social costs and encouraging demoralization and fragmentation amongst the mass of citizens. As yet the labour movement has only begun to regroup its forces and has yet to resume its forward march. Before it can do this we must take the full measure of the impasse that had been reached by the late seventies.

In his original lecture, Hobsbawm relied mainly on broad sociological evidence, such as rates of unionization of the labour force and levels of Labour voting, to substantiate his thesis that the forward march of the labour movement was halted sometime in the fifties. The outcome of the 1979 election, with the Labour vote falling to its lowest point since the 1920s, and the subsequent decline in the strength and membership of trade unions, unable to stem mass unemployment and de-industrialization, have borne out the essentials of Hobsbawm's argument. But there has been another, related sense in which the labour movement has lost momentum in the last two decades. The forward march has been halted not simply because of stagnant or divided support but also because, to extend the image, the maps and equipment available to the marchers command less confidence than ever before, even within Labour's ranks, let alone outside them. On the one hand, the pragmatic ideology of the leaders, a blend of Keynesian demand management and Fabian welfare measures, could no longer deliver the goods; on the other, labour movement activists increasingly defined themselves in terms of immediate struggles and failed to connect those struggles, in any widely understood manner, to the ideal of an alternative social order. There are many reasons for the declining strength of both 'labourist' and socialist ideology: included here would be the resilience of capitalism, and its capacity for fostering consumerism and sectionalism, but also the failures of socialism of every hue, from reformist to revolutionary. The apparent helplessness of Labour governments confronted by capitalist crisis, the alienating bureaucratic procedures associated with Labour's welfare policies, the steady drip of capitalist ideology from the media, the onslaughts of the Thatcherite appeal to individualist opportunism, the petty corruption of those surrounding Wilson and Callaghan, have all helped to discredit the official operating ideology and practical justification of the movement. The fact that the policies of Labour leaders were often opposed from the left does little to rescue the latter from the general debacle. The disappointment of socialism in the East also has a tendency to weaken support for socialism in the West, no matter how strongly the betrayals of Stalinism are repudiated. The collective experience of the very different sorts of failure represented by social democracy in the West and official Communism in the

East has a tendency to breed an indiscriminate cynicism and demoralization. This is not to say that the patient and principled defence of authentic socialist goals is useless or doomed. Rather it means that the objectives of the socialist movement must be elaborated with more precision and imagination than before. Only if this is done will socialists be able to harness the forces of popular resistance that capitalism inevitably and spontaneously provokes.

For many decades socialism in Britain has been drawing on its reserves without sufficiently replenishing them, it has been using up ideas and programmes faster than it has been creating them—it has been 'living on capital' rather than earning its living. We have the advantage in Britain of a workers' movement with a continuous and cumulative tradition stretching back more than a century. The modern socialist and labour movement owes a great deal to the propagation of socialist ideas, ideals and proposals by such organizations as the Social Democratic Federation, the Socialist League, the early Fabian Society, the Independent Labour Party, the Plebs League and the early Communist Party. If one compares the typical pattern of activity of members of these various groupings with that of the contemporary labour movement activist, it emerges that while the former devoted a great deal of energy to socialist education and propaganda, in the broadest and best sense, the latter concentrate most of their attention on the details of trade union policy, wage claims, immediate social problems and their remedies. Today, some educational work goes on inside the relatively small socialist organizations, but very little is directed to a wider public. If one studies the life and work of such different socialists as Morris, Sylvia Pankhurst, Maclean, Tawney, Cole or Dobb it is striking how much they devoted themselves to diffusing socialist ideas, either within the labour movement or within society at large. The non-academic lecturing and writing of socialist publicists made a vital contribution to independent working-class education and to the building of a socialist movement. The organizations and propagandist societies to which they belonged established an organic link to the labour movement and helped to supply it with a distinctive outlook on the world and a vision of a socialist alternative.

In his lecture Eric Hobsbawm briefly refers to the phenomenon of the unionization of white-collar technical and professional workers, and to a certain radicalization of students and intellectuals in the sixties and seventies. This qualifies both the argument that labour's forward march halted in 1950 or thereabouts, and my own reflections on the waning of socialist education and of socialist commitment as such, within the labour movement. In truth there has been a remarkable rebirth of socialist writing and research over the last two decades; Hobsbawm's own work in history, and his contributions to political and theoretical discussion, have themselves exemplified educational influence at work here. For the first time in Britain, Marxism has become a well-established reference point and a fruitful source of inspiration for researchers in history, economics, sociology, cultural studies and many other areas. Margaret Thatcher has been reported as complaining that Marxists now furnish the most widely read interpretations of our national history! Socialist magazines now flourish in many areas of inquiry while initiatives such as the Communist University of London have won respect on the left, and attracted the predictable emnity of the right. As Hobsbawm rightly suggests, the emergence of a stronger socialist intelligentsia in the sixties and seventies has not been without its reverberations in the labour movement. This is, naturally, particularly true of white-collar and public sector unions, a proportion of whose membership is recruited from higher education. Moreover this has happened at a time when white-collar workers and public sector workers have had good reason to consider the wider social and political implications of their work and of their trade union activity. Much of the recent radicalization of the Labour Party reflects a new political awareness amongst the active membership of these unions. To a much more limited extent, the traditional detachments of the organized working class have also been reached by the phenomenon of 'post-sixties' radicalism, via initiatives of the women's movement, radical theatre groups or trade union educational programmes.

However, the emergence of a new socialist culture qualifies, rather than contradicts, the thesis that the labour movement has reached an impasse. The new socialist culture developed mainly in the public education system and has not yet achieved any organized presence within the labour movement—it exists rather as a sort of diffuse, and marginal, influence. While this influence should not be neglected, it certainly falls far short of its potential. The new stratum of 'worker intellectuals' and intellectual workers has helped to sustain some impressive specialist organizations and publications but, so far, nothing to compare with the Plebs League or the Labour Colleges movement. Until recently, many of the characteristic discussions of the new socialist intelligentsia have been remote from the practical problems confronting activists in the labour movement. Today this is changing: socialist intellectuals are more concerned with policy and labour movement activists are less inclined to see sectional economic battles as the key to future advance. But there remains a great deal to be done. It is far from impossible that a Labour government may be elected in the next two or three years committed to a range of left policies: but what should those policies be, and how can their effective implementation be ensured? The Labour Party is currently in the throes of re-making itself and of re-defining its relationship to the wider labour movement. But it is, as yet, far from clear whether this will lead to new frustrations and disappointments, or to a rediscovery of the socialist purpose of the movement. The programme of socialism needs to be renewed to take more adequate account of the nature of capitalism, of the experience of the socialist and labour movement itself, and of major new movements of social emancipation. The development of the women's movement and of feminist theory, the ecological critique of industrialism, the struggle against racism and national oppression, all demand a far-reaching redefinition of socialist programmes. Where the labour movement fails to take up these questions, there has typically been damaging division, or loss of support, as a consequence. Socialism has traditionally aspired to be the programme of a general emancipation from exploitation and oppression; living up to that aspiration is bound to be difficult for socialist and labour movements historically accustomed to relative privilege and male predominance, within an imperial metropolis. On the other hand, with the onset of a new generalized recession within the capitalist world, and of a special crisis of the archaic forms of the British state, going on in the old way will also be painful, both for the old and the new sections of the working class. Within a society afflicted by demoralization and decay, social crisis and destructive individualism, the fundamental ideas of socialism retain all their validity and are an indispensable source of guidance and inspiration for a vigorous and healthy labour movement. That is why it is now urgently necessary to rediscover the commitment to socialist research and education that helped to shape the early labour movement. Together with the new priorities indicated above, any movement for the renewal of socialist programmes today will have to be more attuned to strictly *political* questions, concerning the organization of the state, than was the case with the early labour movement. The early socialists possessed an acute social insight but paid less attention to the forms of the state itself. In the high noon of Victorian imperialism the latter was, in any case, a most imposing edifice. Today, the form of the British state—of the 'United Kingdom' with its monarchy, House of Lords, judiciary, security forces, and restive or recalcitrant national components—is probably more vulnerable than it was then. The labour and socialist movement has proceeded for over a century within a larger political structure that, at its centre, seemed impervious to change; indeed the stability of that structure made it easier for a unified and cumulative tradition of working class organization to develop. Now that the structures of the politics have been called into question, the labour movement, even to survive, will have to redefine its relations to it in far-reaching ways. Going on in the old 'Labourist' way, as a corporation within the body politic, is no longer a viable option. Labour cannot stand still. It must either move forward against the power of capital, and its political guarantees, or suffer the destruction of its remaining political influence and of the popular conquests it has helped to realize.

4

Observations on the Debate

Eric Hobsbawm

This book, like the earlier discussion in *Marxism Today* and elsewhere has grown out of a lecture by an academic historian some three years ago. The debate has mobilized not merely other academic intellectuals, which is common enough, but people involved at all levels in political and trade union activity, from local branch to parliament, and from the workshop floor to national leaders. We all find ourselves between the covers of the same book. This does not happen often, for theory and practice, the writers and the doers, are not as easily combined as they ought to be. The first point I would like to make, before taking up the issues raised in the debate since it was provisionally concluded in *Marxism Today* in 1979, is that this shows that theory does not have to be imprisoned in the overheated aquarium in which intellectual specialists swim about like some sort of tropical fish. Some theory does not confine itself to dealing with the real world as we know it, and with the palpable problems and tasks that confront those of us who want to improve and change it. But when theory faces this world and these tasks, the screen that divides those whose business is writing from the rest disappears. We all take the same language and contribute to the discussion.

As for the main subject of this debate, nobody can seriously deny that the British labour movement today is in a considerable mess. It is in a state of deeper crisis and confusion than was easily foreseeable even three years ago. To this extent the basic argument of 'The Forward March of Labour Halted?' is not easily challenged, and in fact none of the new contributors to the debate have disagreed with it. Wherever the march of labour is going to take us in future, it has certainly not taken us forward since 1978. It has brought electoral defeat, followed by what is probably the most reactionary government of Britain this century, and certainly (barring Turkey) the most reactionary government in Europe at the present moment. It is also a spectacularly disastrous government, which has intensified the British part of the global capitalist crisis to the point where it is, almost certainly, already worse than the crisis of 1929–33[1]—which is not the case in other capitalist countries. Few workers who voted for Thatcher don't bitterly regret doing so, and even large sections of British capitalists are desperately looking for someone else to back. In the circumstances one would expect a major surge of support for Labour, led by a united labour movement confident of victory.

Instead we find a confused and divided labour movement, torn by splits and internal squabbles, and isolated from many of its old supporters. Halfway through the course of a disastrous and deeply unpopular government in which nobody in Britain or abroad believes—not even most of its members—belief in Labour as an alternative government had also slumped. That at such a time one of the most solid Labour constituencies in England could almost be lost to the candidate of a third party that did not even pretend to put forward an alternative policy, and to a man personally associated with the EEC, which is certainly not a popular cause, amounts to a popular vote of no confidence in Labour. It is not to be explained away. So long as this situation lasts it would be absurd to claim that labour has resumed its forward march, or looks like doing so.

While this is so, it is still as vital as it was three years ago to analyse dispassionately what has brought Labour to the present pass. There can be no reversal of Labour's fortunes, unless, in

---

[1] Unemployment is already comparable to 1929–33 and will go on rising. Unlike the 1930s, the framework of British social welfare is being simultaneously dismantled—e.g. schools and health service—while public and private housebuilding, which were then booming, have virtually ceased. The structure of British productive industry is being demolished almost beyond the hope of restoration.

the words of Jack Jones, we 'avoid a repetition of slogans and generalizations from the past, allied with a refusal to assess realistically the facts of the present'. Are all the contributors to the present discussion ready to accept the facts of the situation and the results of a realistic diagnosis? I am not so sure.

In this instance the facts are too strong to be denied. Two apparent indications of labour advance have been or may be mentioned: British unions (as Steve Jefferys was right to point out) began to increase their membership again in the 1970s after a quarter-century of stagnation, and it may be that Labour Party membership has also lately begun to rise. As against this, the signs of decay accumulate. The national Labour vote forms a lower percentage of the electorate than at any time since 1931. In absolute figures it has inexorably drifted down from its peak of almost 14 millions in 1951 to 11.5 millions in 1979, except for a brief rise in 1964–6. If people don't vote Labour, there can be no Labour government, a fact sometimes overlooked by enthusiastic militants. The parties and groups to the left of the Labour Party have no significant electorate, national or even local. The Labour Party itself, in terms of its individual active membership, is not at present a mass party, even allowing for a recent influx of activists. It is probably less of a mass party at the moment than the Conservatives. Nobody can claim that the Communist Party and other Marxist parties and organizations are expanding significantly. The political radicalization of a section of the young after 1968 has not continued. At a representative meeting of perhaps 150 assorted leftwing intellectuals in the spring of 1981 there was not a single person under twenty-five. As for the unions, their power and capacity to resist attacks upon them remains, in spite of all, the most impressive part of the labour movement. Nevertheless their relative strength underlines the *political* weakness of the movement. For the first time since 1923 the national Labour electorate is today *smaller* than the number of unionists affiliated to the TUC: even in the disastrous year of 1931 it was larger. But if Labour today can mobilize no larger numbers than the TUC can organize, it cannot mobilize even the members of the trade union movement for its cause. In 1979 one-third of unionists actually seem to have voted Tory; and if the Warrington election is any guide, if they won't vote for the Tories, many of them won't vote for Labour any longer.

A few years ago it was this contrast between a declining and uncertain political labour movement and a growing, militant and apparently unbeatable industrial movement capable of resisting and defeating governments which encouraged a good many illusions about its political potential. If we use the metaphor that Raymond Williams rightly challenges, people acted as though the bird of labour could fly on one wing, and indeed they were sometimes tempted to argue that the political wing could somehow be regenerated by the flapping of the industrial one. These illusions, which were accompanied by a certain idealization of rank-and-file action as such, are not entirely dead, since they are based on the perfectly true observation that 'organization from below' (Jefferys) is a necessary part of any political as well as industrial strategy of the left. But it is not enough to say that the road to Labour's recovery is to be found simply by 'really working on the basics: the respect of picket lines, collections for others on strike, solidarity action, rebuilding the independence of the shop-stewards' committees, building united rank-and-file organizations to generalize the anti-Tory fight' (Jefferys). Important as all these tasks are, they are not enough.

Nor can the great illusion of the 1970s, that militant unionism is enough, be saved by arguing that it would have been enough if only the unions had not been so narrow-minded: if we had not 'failed to harness the rank-and-file strength of the movement to clear class-wide socialist perspectives' (Jefferys), or if unions had not 'neglected to be political in the sense of campaigning around the wider social needs of working people and other oppressed groups' (Wainwright). Certainly there could have been more harnessing and broader campaigning, though the need for both is not exactly a new discovery among socialists. But it is clear from the arguments of both Jefferys and Wainwright that the strength of militancy is 'not sufficient in the face of a world capitalist crisis and a Britain dominated by multinational capital' (Jefferys), and that the power of unions *by itself*, is essentially 'the power to bargain over the employment contract' (Wainwright)—one might add, on behalf of particular groups of workers. However much union action is widened politically, it therefore can only be *one part* of labour's struggle, though a fundamental, crucial and formidable part. Inevitably there is much of vital interest to workers as citizens, and to citizens not directly represented by unions, that industrial action cannot at most times deal with adequately or at all, and which must be fought for in other ways. Of course everyone recognizes this in principle, and (except for syndicalists) has done so ever since British unions, over eighty years ago, recognized that they needed a party, including the socialists, to supplement their action. It is certainly recognized today. Nevertheless, in practice, the temptation to think in purely industrial terms appears not to have been entirely overcome.

This temptation also leads people to underestimate or explain away possible contradictions within the industrial sector of the movement and frictions between unions and other parts of the movement. Most of the debate on 'The Forward March' has dealt with one aspect of these difficulties, namely trade union sectionalism. I do not want to prolong this debate, since *in practice* three things seem to be widely accepted by the participants. First, it is clear that sectionalism raises very serious problems, whether or not it has recently increased. Second, it is clear, not least from Jack Jones's valuable—and, coming from him, pretty authoritative—contribution, that there is no *automatic* way of spiriting away the differences between trade unions and the Labour Party, which developed over the years and still exist particularly in times of Labour government. A concrete and limited set of policy objectives has to be hammered out to which both sides have to be committed, even when it does not represent what each would want if left to itself. And third, some contributors admit the unpalatable but undeniable fact 'that resentment towards trade union power has in fact grown' (Wainwright), even among supporters of Labour and probably within the membership of unions. We cannot pretend that this did not influence the defeat of the Labour government in 1979 or, because such resentment has paradoxically continued even as trade union power has declined in a time of slump and unemployment, that it is not still a significant political factor.

We might argue about a great many matters. Thus I belive that Jack Jones is right against Hilary Wainwright in his analysis of the political failures of the movement in the 1970s. The fault of the unions was not to look to Labour governments and councils to meet 'all the workers' other needs' beyond those with which collective bargaining can deal directly, and *therefore* limit themselves 'to fighting for the interests of the wage earners, full stop.' In itself this is sensible enough, since union action *alone* can achieve only limited, though indispensable, aims. Unions can, by their capacity to mobilize workers, greatly assist in wider campaigns, and by their peculiar position in the Labour Party, help to shape the policy of Labour governments. Unions can, as the most massive form of citizens' self-organization, broaden the horizons of what we think of as 'politics' beyond the institutional and parliamentary or other representative (i.e. indirect) forms of political action, which act for and on behalf of (and sometimes against) people, but only occasionally allow them to act *for themselves*. But they cannot replace the wider political movement of labour, of which they are only one part, though a crucial one. There must be some 'division of labour'. The fault of both unions and party in the period when there was a 'deepening division between the Labour Party leadership and the trade union movement' was that—in spite of efforts to the contrary by people like Jones—Labour leaders carried out a policy that workers did not expect from their party, and trade unions in turn pursued their own narrow interests irrespective of government, including Labour governments, and thus helped to bring both Conservative and Labour governments to defeat.

However, though there is much more to be said about sectionalism and other problems of the trade unions, and several arguments in some of the new contributions on which I would reserve the right to disagree, other aspects of Labour's difficulties are equally and perhaps more urgent. They have not emerged so clearly from the discussion to date.

Since 1979 the illusion of salvation through union militancy has been replaced by another, and probably more dangerous set of illusions, based on the fact that the only dynamic aspect of the movement of late has been the striking advance of the left within the organizations of the Labour Party. This is indeed a most impressive and welcome phenomenon. The present position of the left in the party, based on its strength and planned organization among activists in constituency parties and unions, and on constitutional changes such as the reselection of candidates and the new method of electing the party's leaders, would have been quite inconceivable even ten years ago. The next Labour victory, it is hoped, will bring into office a parliamentary majority of the left, under socialist leadership, and not only committed to a socialist policy by the party manifesto as formulated by Conference, but no longer able to deviate from it once the new Labour government is in being. But, it is assumed that the party's turn to the left and its promise of staying true to its commitment, will itself guarantee the next Labour victory.

This illusion is more dangerous than that of the 1970s, because it entirely by-passes the main problem, which is that the best and most left-wing party is not enough, if the masses won't support it in sufficient numbers. Old and new Marxists in Britain unfortunately have plenty of experience of this. Trade unionism, with all its limitations, was never able to overlook the masses, because it organizes millions of them, and has to represent them all the time and mobilize them quite a lot of the time. But capturing the Labour Party for the left can be done in the short run without reference to them. It could in theory be achieved pretty well entirely by a smallish minority of a few tens of thousands of committed socialists and left Labour people by means of meetings, drafting resolutions and votes. The illusion of the early 1980s is that *organization* can replace politics. There are today several tens of thousands of such activists, and their numbers are increasing, because the successes of the left within the party encourage their hope. They are tempted, as I suggested to Tony Benn (see p. 97) to look at the problem of resuming Labour's forward march 'in a little too narrow an organizational sense'.

But they are tempted to overlook—until electoral disaster

dramatizes their oversight—the basic problem: how to get the British peoples, who reject Thatcherism utterly, to turn to Labour again. This they are visibly not doing at present, in spite of the fact that Labour is not only the party of the working people but the obvious alternative party of government.

There are three aspects of this problem. We need to analyse first, what the basis of the forward march of Labour was between 1900 and the 1950s, and whether this basis is still sufficient to ensure its resumption. Second, we need to analyse the reasons for the decline in the political support for Labour, particularly in the past fifteen years. And third, we need to consider *politically* the ways of reversing this trend.

Basically Labour grew and became a party of government as what its name said it was, the party of the manual working class, conscious that it needed a political class party. Most studies of why people vote Labour have come to essentially the same conclusion as McKenzie and Silver in 1968: 'When working-class Labour voters were asked what the parties were "like" they tended overwhelmingly to reply in terms of class'; or Westergaard and Resler: 'Asked why they vote as they do, manual working-class Labour supporters usually refer to the fact that the party is—or is supposed to be—the party of the working class.' For most of this century the manual workers formed a substantial majority of the British peoples, but while for half a century workers increasingly moved towards their class party, even at the peak of Labour's fortunes (1945–1966) between thirty-five and forty per cent of them did not (yet) vote for the Labour Party. The decline in Labour's fortunes after 1951 was thus, at least initially, not to be explained by a numerical decline in the manual proletariat.

Nevertheless, Labour rose not only as a party of manual workers. It appealed disproportionately to the minority peoples of Britain, not only because Scotland and Wales were proportionately more industrialized than England and the Irish in Britain were overwhelmingly workers, but also because the Scots, Welsh and Irish are minority peoples. It also appealed to a small but growing section of intellectuals and 'progressive' middle strata, as the heir of a defunct liberal-radicalism, the party of education, reason and progress, of a more socially just society, and largely as the party of peace. This was perhaps not of major electoral significance even in 1945, but the move 'forward from Liberalism' is nevertheless not negligible, as witness the political history of families such as the Foots and the (Wedgwood) Benns. More significant was the turn of a growing number of the small salaried white-collar and lower professional employees to Labour, which became notable in 1945 for these groups (with some exceptions such as teachers) had previously kept aloof from the workers. In short, Labour also rose as a potential or actual 'people's party' of progressive change.

But there is a third element. Since 1918 the party has been committed to a socialist objective, and pretty certainly most working-class Labour supporters have also believed, however imprecisely, that capitalism ought to end and a newer and better society, should replace it, and not only a less unfair version of the present society. To this extent the British working class in politics, unlike the US working class, became— and one hopes has remained—socialist. The historians who have underestimated this aspect of Labour's rise, especially between 1918 and 1945, are mistaken. The argument of the Labour right, that Clause 4 was electorally damaging, was both disingenuous and wrong. It was bogus, because the right rejected the socialism of Clause 4 anyway, and not just because they thought it would lose votes; and it was wrong because it has not prevented Labour from winning general elections since the 1950s. Nor will it. On the contrary, it may be argued that Labour's greatest leaps forward have taken place when it was carried by great surges of hope for a better society, as in 1945 when the Labour vote rose by almost 50 per cent.[2] Nor

---

[2] Let us remember what happened in 1945. The Tory or coalition vote remained almost stable compared with 1935 (10.7 millions against 11.4 millions), the Liberal vote rose substantially (from 1.4 to 2.2 millions). The total electorate had increased by 8 per cent. Labour's rise from 8.5 to 12 millions was therefore not due to a swing from the old parties, but to a flood of previous non-voters and of first-time voters. And this under a bad electoral register, and with 40 per cent of the forces unable to vote.

has or will the hope of a transformed Britain appeal only to manual workers. On the contrary, at a time of national crisis, almost of national despair, it can have the widest appeal.

Now the original basis of Labour's forward march was weakened. The manual working class of the old kind is now probably a minority and certainly a diminishing proportion of the people. So, even if we suppose that all the old working-class supporters flock back to the party, we would not get back to 1945. And while the 'new' working class of white-collar, technical and lesser professional employees is now indeed largely organized in unions, and a part of them (especially in the public sector) have undoubtedly been radicalized, their 'class consciousness' is not necessarily the same as that of the old-style manual workers and their spontaneous attraction to a 'party of the working class' is less. It is a safe bet that the percentage of ASTMS members who vote Labour is smaller than that of NUR and ASLEF members, even though the leadership of ASTMS is further to the left than that of the other two.

Moreover, even the 'old' working class is no longer what it was a generation ago, quite apart from the changes in its composition which my original article attempted to sketch. In general, as Jack Adams rightly points out, 'mass support for political advance and the assertion of class consciousness . . . have waned . . . Among elderly people I frequently find a sympathetic response and a clear class understanding in discussion. These are less strong in later generations, although many young people are evidently looking for a radical alternative.' More specifically, there have been changes that discourage the old type of political consciousness. Thus the values of consumer-society individualism and the search for private and personal satisfactions above all else, have been daily taken into every living-room for a generation by the media (Adams is right to draw attention to the media, but I would stress not so much the distortions and bias of news and propaganda, as the constant atmosphere of apparently unpolitical advertising and entertainment breathed in by all of us). Moreover, the weakening of the hold of the old labour movement itself has made some workers less resistant to reactionary infections such as racism.

For good or ill, we cannot simply go back to what Steve Jefferys rather offensively calls 'the Andy Capp class consciousness' of the 1940s. Incidentally, I never suggested that we could, though, with all my reservations about it, I regret it.

Moreover, we cannot simply expect the old calls for socialism to have the same resonance as in the past. Not many people today look to the various socialist countries as models for a socialist Britain, or are inspired by them as British workers once were by what they saw as 'the first workers' state' in the Soviet Union.[3] After thirty to forty years of living with many nationalized industries, the call to nationalize some more may indeed be valid and necessary, but it no longer looks like an automatic solution to the workers' problems, as it did when Will Lawther proclaimed in 1944: 'What could be achieved through public ownership? It would win the complete confidence of the miners and their families. Generations of suspicion and hatred would be wiped out, and an entirely new attitude developed towards the coal industry.' The case for socialism is as strong as ever, but it has to be argued in a new way, with much clearer proposals concerning the sort of society we want and what socialism can achieve, rather than a repetition of old slogans which, however valid, no longer carry the same conviction. This point is rightly and forcefully made by Robin Blackburn. We cannot rely on our past.

These observations are enough to throw doubt on the proposition that all that stands between us and the next Labour government is a good left-wing programme for Labour and the proof that the party programme will not be betrayed. However, the view that this is the master-key to a resumption of Labour's forward march is based on a more specific diagnosis of Labour's defeat and crisis, which is mistaken. With the one exception of 1966 the Labour vote has continued to fall inexorably since 1951. The Party has lost or won elections not because of the movement of its own support, but because of those of the Tory and other party votes. Labour won in 1964 because the Tory vote

[3] Even the right-wing Labour Executive, in a scathing report on *British Labour and Communism* in the 1930s, felt constrained to pay tribute to the achievements of the Russian Revolution.

fell by 1.7 millions, lost in 1970 because it rose by about the same number, won in February 1974 because it fell by over a million, and in October 1974 by about the same, and lost in 1979 because the Tories' vote increased by over 3 millions. Third party votes also went up and down like yo-yos. Labour's own vote did not vary by more than a couple of hundred thousand between elections (omitting 1966),[4] drifting downwards all the time.

Whatever happened to Labour in the 1970s was clearly not due to dramatic reactions of the mass of *actual* Labour voters to Labour or other governments, but to the reactions of people who ought perhaps to have been Labour voters, *but no longer were*. Labour governments have not been defeated because of secessions of Labour voters disappointed with their record: in 1951 2 million more voted for Labour than in 1945, and even in 1979 the Callaghan government lost with a shade *more* votes than it had won with in 1974.[5] This reduces much talk about the reasons for Labour's defeats through the betrayal of programmes to folklore. But there is one significant exception: the Wilson years of 1964–70. Here, and here alone we have a *rise* of 0.8 million in the Labour vote (1966), followed by a big *fall* of a little more than this (1970). Why?

At no time did the Wilson governments have a programme worth the name, and hence they could hardly betray it. Labour got a majority because it offered the hope of change, and it lost, not only because, like all governments since then, it proved incapable of coping with the crisis of the British economy, but also because it did very nearly the opposite of what Labour voters and trade unionists expected from a Labour government. There is no denying the disappointment and demoralization of traditional Labour supporters. But once again, the crux of the problem lay not in the 'solid' Labour vote, which hardly changed between 1964 and 1970, but in the failure to seize the 1966 opportunity to widen Labour's support again, and even to hold the support then temporarily gained. Labour's forward

[4] Except, curiously, when it just nosed ahead of the Tories in February 1974 with half a million fewer votes than in the year of defeat, 1970.

[5] The really massive drop in the Labour vote—1.5 millions—occurred during the Tory and cold-war years of 1951–55, and must be explained differently.

march cannot be resumed so long as we think primarily in terms of people like those who form the large but declining block of men and women who are still within the field of the old loyalties, appeals, discourses and arguments of 'the movement', and, still less, of the devoted minority of activists. A vast mass of potential Labour voters, even among the members of the trade unions, no longer are.

How is it to be resumed? That it can be done is proved by the recent examples of parties that have succeeded, at least for a time, in breaking out of the stagnation, decline and political isolation which is not confined to British Labour. But it has been done by parties that have moved forward not *only* as class parties, and still less as sectional pressure groups and alliances of minority interests, but as 'people's parties' with which the majority of their nation interested in progressive reform and change can identify; as spokesman for the nation in time of crisis. This does not mean that they cease to be based on the labour movement. Unity between Socialists and Communists, insisted on against opposition within and outside the French Socialist Party and underlined by Communist participation in President Mitterand's government, was the essential condition of its triumph. Nor does it mean that such a party retreats from its programme. The French Socialist Party won an absolute majority with a programme to the left of anything so far suggested by the British Labour left. The Labour Party is potentially such a party. It must learn again to act like one.

This means that it should be and act as what Tony Benn himself sees as the first condition of Labour's revival (see p. 89 above), namely, 'a broad party' leading a broad movement. This does not merely mean a recognition of diversity within the party, but of the diversity of the classes and other groups of the population, of the aspirations and interests of those who make up the broad progressive front that must carry Labour to victory. This means not only that both left and right, however embattled, belong to a broad movement and have a right to be there, something that has been more readily recognized in the trade union movement than in the Labour Party. Terry Duffy and Tom Jackson are labour leaders as much as Alan Fisher,

Arthur Scargill and Ken Gill; they represent genuine currents of opinion within the movement, however much we may wish to change such opinions; and the movement as a whole would be weakened if the right or the left seceded.

But it also means that we must distinguish clearly between individual figures and bodies of opinion. I do not suppose anyone of the left grieves for those right-wing individuals who have, over the years, left the party and found a more congenial as well as presumably a more prosperous home elsewhere—the Shawcrosses, Robenses, and the rest. I do not suppose that the loss of Roy Jenkins as a person, was much regretted. But it is a mistake to dismiss the collective secession of the Social Democrats and the foundation of a new party as good riddance. It represents the loss of a significant section of the left-of-centre middle class, which long looked to Labour, and in many cases actively worked for Labour *rather than* some other party. As is now clear, it potentially represents a significant electoral weakening of the Labour Party—how much is still unclear. In short, it represents a lot of people who ought to support the Labour Party, and who must again be won for it, whatever we think of the Gang of Four. And anyone who thinks a Labour Party without such supporters will at least be a stronger, more committed and united force for socialism, should pause. Both as a historian and as a Marxist whose political memory goes back half a century, I have known plenty of strong, committed parties, great, small and tiny, with admirable programmes, which have never built socialism or even been in government, except as occasional parts of coalitions in which they were much more shackled by their bourgeois partners than supporters of Benn need be by having to coexist with supporters of Healey. Moreover, the experience of the left unfortunately suggests that in these days even a committed socialist party will not escape internal divisions and quarrels.

As Jack Jones reminds us, the party that will resume Labour's forward march must think of politics in terms of ordinary people inside and outside the movement, and not primarily in terms of the activists who are untypical, if only because they spend far more time and energy on the movement than most men and women. We may or may not agree with Jones about the Social Contract, but he is surely right in stressing, time and again, that we need policies 'that workers can understand and fight for'; that it is disastrous when a Labour leadership does not put forward 'policies with much impact on working class opinion', that 'because much of the critical work now going on is of the academic intellectual variety, there is not much understanding among the trade union rank and file about what has to be done'; that 'workers need to see and feel progress to gain confidence', that 'you gain mass interest by fighting for things that people see as justified and feasible'. Perhaps Jones concentrates a bit too much on the (necessary) campaigns around 'simple, clear, limited policies' which can be seen to bring immediate advantage. People want not only jobs for school-leavers, but a fairer and better world for their children, and confidence in a party which will work for it, beyond any immediate programme. And Labour needs to appeal not only to working people but to all who need such a better and fairer world. Yet, fundamentally, Jones is right.

The future of Labour and the advance to socialism depends on mobilizing people who remember the date of the Beatles' break-up and not the date of the Saltley pickets; of people who have never read *Tribune* and who do not care a damn about the deputy-leadership of the Labour Party, except (if they are Labour supporters) insofar as they are troubled by the fact that, as Britain founders after over two years of Thatcherism, the party seems to spend so much of its time on mutual laceration. They may be wrong, but the reason why these struggles are not just remote and incomprehensible has not been explained to their satisfaction. The future of Labour and socialism depends on men and women, blue-collar, white-collar and no collar, ranging from zero CSE to PhD, who are, regrettably, not revolutionaries, even though they want a new and better Britain and, if they can be shown that socialism can achieve this, a socialist Britain. In this century Labour has advanced with the support of such people, who have accepted the leadership of the left when it has made sense to them in their own terms. If Labour is to advance again, it cannot forget this.

For if such people do not vote for Labour—which is the minimal index of political support—then Labour will not reverse its long-term decline.

There are only three possible ways of avoiding this conclusion. We may suppose that there is still a huge mass of men and women identified with 'the movement' who will automatically support *any* leadership and *any* policy because it represents Labour, when it comes to the point of voting. We would be unwise any longer to rely on this, however: millions will still stay loyal, come what may, but they will not be enough. We may also suppose that somewhere there is a vast, unknown, untapped reservoir of left votes. There is no good evidence for this view at present. Lastly we may put our money on a breakdown of British capitalism and politics, leading to a crisis in which the masses will turn to the left. Since we are in such a crisis, in which British capitalism *is* breaking down, and since traditional politics and the system of class rule are visibly unable to carry on in the old ways, this is not an implausible scenario. But if this crisis has hitherto shown anything, it is that the masses have so far not turned to Labour or the left, or are likely to do so automatically.

Labour could still form the next government, if the curious British electoral system, even with a declining Labour vote, produces a parliamentary majority because the anti-Labour vote is sufficiently split between Tories, Liberals, Social Democrats and whoever else. No doubt the politicians, commentators and swingometrists are already busy figuring out possibilities on their pocket calculators. In such circumstances, a committed Labour government could still achieve much. But let us make no mistake. In such circumstances the problems of reversing Labour's decline and resuming its forward march would not have been solved, or even tackled. The task would still be there to face us. And we would have no excuses left if we failed.

© *1981, E.J. Hobsbawm*

**also available
in Verso paperback editions**

Wolfgang Abendroth
A Short History of the European Working Class
£2.00 (NLB)

Perry Anderson
Arguments Within English Marxism
£4.25

Michèle Barrett
Women's Oppression Today*
£3.95

Regis Debray
Conversations With Allende
£1.05 (NLB)

Ernest Mandel
Late Capitalism
£5.75

The Second Slump*
£2.95

Revolutionry Marxism Today*
£4.75

Roy Medvedev
Leninism and Western Socialism*
£4.50

Tom Nairn
The Break-Up of Britain*
new edition, £4.95

/over

Riccardo Parboni
The Dollar and Its Rivals*
£3.95

Göran Therborn
What Does the Ruling Class Do When It Rules?
£4.50

Raymond Williams
Problems in Materialism and Culture*
£3.95

Politics and Letters*
£4.50

*NLB hardcover available

LIBRARY OF DAVIDSON COLLEGE

for **two weeks.** Books
renewed.